The Bloc

Manon Cornellier

Translated by Robert Chodos,
Simon Horn, and Wanda Taylor

James Lorimer & Company, Publishers
Toronto 1995

James Lorimer & Company Ltd. acknowledges with thanks the support of the Canada Council, the Ontario Arts Council, and the Ontario Publishing Centre in the development of writing and publishing in Canada.

Cover photo of Lucien Bouchard by Jacques Boissinot/CP Photo.

Canadian Cataloguing in Publication Data

Cornellier, Manon
    The Bloc

Issued also in French under title: Le Bloc.
    ISBN 1-55028-473-8 (bound) ISBN 1-55028-472-X (pbk.)

Bloc-quebecois. 2. Bouchard, Lucien, 1938-
3. Quebec (Province) - History - Autonomy and independence movements. 4. Canada - Politics and government - 1993-   .* 5. Quebec - Politics and government - 1985-   .* I. Title.

Jl197.B56C6713 1995 324.271'098 C95-931882-8

James Lorimer & Company, Publishers
35 Britain Street
Toronto, Ontario
M5A 1R7

Printed and bound in Canada

Contents

Acknowledgements

If this book finally exists, it is because a number of people offered me support and encouragement. I would like especially to thank all the people who agreed to be interviewed, in particular Lucien Bouchard and his staff.

I would like to express my thanks as well to Jean-Marc Léger and his polling firm, Léger & Léger, who graciously offered polling data to me for use in the book. I would like to note the marvellous cooperation offered, always with a smile, by the staff of a great institution, the Canadian Parliamentary Library. I would also like to mention the help of Normand Sceay, the director of the Bloc's documentation centre, who let me go through piles of documents.

I would like to thank Bob Chodos, Simon Horn, and Wanda Taylor for their skilful translation of the French text into English.

Finally, I would like to express my deepest gratitude to Diane Young, of James Lorimer & Company, who, with her advice and detailed review of the manuscript, made the publication of this book possible.

Introduction

On June 15, 1991, the college gymnasium in Tracy, Quebec was jammed with enthusiastic political activists who had come from all over the province to create a new political party, the Bloc Québécois, a sovereignist party that would operate at the federal level. Nobody knew at the time what to expect. Would it survive? Would it overcome the prevailing scepticism? Would it become one of the driving forces of the sovereignty movement? Would it be seen in English Canada as a threat? A federal election was still two or three years down the road. With only eight MPs, no money, and no members, the future should have looked grim. But the polls were reassuring, and the participants had the feeling they were on a historic road.

Their dream was not new. The desire of Quebecers and French Canadians to go to Ottawa to defend their different vision of the country is almost as old as Canada itself. In fact, there has been a long line of Quebec politicians who have believed they could do more for their country or province by remaining independent of the major parties. The pioneers were Charles Anger and Olivar Asselin who in 1900 tried unsuccessfully to enter Parliament as independent nationalists. They wanted to protest against Liberal Prime Minister Sir Wilfrid Laurier's 1899 decision to finance volunteers to go and fight alongside British forces in the Boer War in South Africa. The two men, who were associates of Henri Bourassa, were essentially Canadian nationalists. They favoured a policy of Canadian independence and opposed British imperialism.

It was not until the Second World War and the Conscription Crisis that candidates ran openly in federal elections as French Canadian, rather than Canadian, nationalists. The catalyst was the plebiscite called by Prime Minister Mackenzie King, in response to pressure from some English Canadian groups and the Conservative opposition, to release him from a vow made to Quebec in 1939. To win voter support, the Liberal Party had promised not to impose conscription for military service in Europe. The plebiscite was held in 1942.

As expected, 80 per cent of English Canadians voted to release King from his promise, while in Quebec 71.2 per cent voted to hold him to it. Among Francophones, 85 per cent rejected King's request. The country was split in two.[1] Quebecers were outraged. Nationalists, led by journalist André Laurendeau, responded by setting up the Bloc Populaire. The Bloc Populaire initially became active on the provincial scene, but then gained its first federal seat when J.A. Choquette won a byelection in the riding of Stanstead on August 9, 1943.

King did impose compulsory military service, but gradually, and it was not until 1944 that conscripts were sent to the battlefields of Europe. Nonetheless, the resentment endured. In the 1945 general election, a number of independents were elected in Quebec, but the election was a defeat for the Bloc Populaire. Although it won 13.1 per cent of the popular vote in Quebec, only two of its candidates were elected — J.J. Hamel in Saint-Maurice–Laflèche and Maxime Raymond in Beauharnois-Laprairie.[2] Formed for a specific reason, the Bloc Populaire did not last long. It had disappeared by the next election.

The rise of the independence movement in the 1960s and 1970s revived the debate about nationalist representation in Parliament. As each federal election came around, the issue returned to haunt the sovereignists. They didn't know whether they should abstain, support a third party or field their own candidates. For a number of years, many nationalists supported populist politician Réal Caouette, leader of the Ralliement des Créditistes, because of his concern for Quebec's interests.

During the 1970s, the Parti Québécois (PQ) took on the task of issuing instructions as to what its supporters should do in federal elections — with mixed results, however, as the instructions changed each time. This process began in earnest during the 1974 federal election. The PQ National Council recommended what it considered "the only politically logical solution," which was that people abstain or spoil their ballots. The party spent $25,000 on an advertising campaign. Nine million postage-stamp-sized seals were printed. Buttons and 150,000 stickers were distributed to spread the message. This policy created a sense of unease in some riding associations that were close to the union movement and the NDP. A number of organizers decided not to follow the party's instructions. Some supported the New Democrats, while others backed the Créditistes.[3]

In 1979 and 1980, the PQ once again failed to receive unanimous support when it urged its members to vote for the Créditistes. The

PQ hoped that by supporting the Créditistes, it could hinder the Liberals in Quebec and give a helping hand to Joe Clark's Conservatives, who had no base in the province. The PQ leadership felt this was the best scenario leading up to the referendum on sovereignty-association. But the strategy failed.[4] A small group of sovereignists rejected the strategy immediately and decided to form their own party, the Union Populaire. Even without official support, they succeeded in fielding enough candidates to obtain party status under the Elections Act.

In the 1984 federal election, the PQ was more divided than ever. One group advocated support for a federal party, while another favoured forming a federal wing of the Parti Québécois. This debate, which raged in PQ ranks for more than two years, marked a turning point in the party's history.

In October 1981, at the PQ National Council in Jonquière, René Lévesque announced to reporters that his party was planning to form a federal wing, an idea already championed by his environment minister, Marcel Léger. In the months that followed, frustration grew among pro-independence forces. The first ministers' conference held in Ottawa in early November concluded with a slap in the face to Quebec. Justice Minister Jean Chrétien and the premiers of the other nine provinces succeeded in concocting an agreement on the repatriation of the constitution, a new amending formula and a Charter of Rights. Not only was Quebec excluded from the final negotiations, but its traditional constitutional demands were either swept under the carpet or rejected.

On December 6, 1981, the Parti Québécois held its eighth congress. The atmosphere was tense. The preceding Wednesday, Prime Minister Pierre Elliott Trudeau had presented his plan to repatriate the constitution to the House of Commons. Marcel Léger, the party's highly popular organizer, brought up the idea of a federal wing. He was supported by trade unionist Michel Bourdon, today a PQ MNA. By a vote of more than 900 to 615, delegates decided to continue examining the possibility of PQ participation in a federal election, including fielding candidates if necessary.[5]

During the same period, another independence supporter, University of Montreal political science professor Denis Monière, published a book suggesting that the PQ form a federal wing. Some people took up the idea from the start while others were drawn to the suggestion but then backed off.

And so the issue dragged on. Secret PQ polls showed that a nationalist party would have a good chance of success. But PQ MNAs and the Cabinet remained divided. Then in June 1982, the PQ set up a task force to study the proposal for a federal party, but the idea of supporting "good candidates" from the other parties, especially the Conservatives, had made inroads among those who wanted revenge on the federal Liberals for the repatriation of the Constitution. "The backroom work done by the former Conservatives in the party began to produce results," Marcel Léger later wrote.[6] In the late summer of 1982, René Lévesque started to back away from the proposal. He told Léger that he considered the launch of a federal party to be premature. Yet the idea was taking root among activists.[7] In October, consultation by the party leadership revealed that approximately seventy ridings would be in favour of a federal party.

Marcel Léger, no longer a cabinet member, continued his organizational efforts. However, he felt that the battle was not yet won and launched a public campaign in the newspapers, but without success.[8] With the support of some of his big guns, Lévesque succeeded in turning the party around. On October 31, 1982, the National Council decided it would participate in the next federal election, but without necessarily creating a federal wing of the PQ. In his 1986 book, Marcel Léger maintained that because he was excluded from the Cabinet from 1982 on, he did not know about the existence of a group whose core members were Conservative allies. This group wanted to "nip in the bud any possibility in 1982 of a group of sovereignists making a breakthrough on the federal scene. They wanted to change the political dynamics within the Parti Québécois, and help the Conservatives in Ottawa."[9]

In the summer of 1983, a number of PQ members decided to form a party that would be legally independent of the PQ. Under the leadership of Marcel Léger and Denis Monière, the Parti Nationaliste (PN) was officially established in mid-September, a few short months after Lucien Bouchard's close friend Brian Mulroney was chosen leader of the Conservative Party. In October, PQ activists agreed to recognize the PN as their "means of political intervention on the federal scene."[10] But the disenchantment prevailing among pro-independence forces and the PQ's growing unpopularity put the PN at a disadvantage. The PN did not have the favourable political circumstances that the Bloc Québécois would enjoy a few years later. In the 1984 federal election, the Conservatives swept Quebec, winning fifty-eight of its seventy-five seats. Among the elected Conservatives were thirty or so nationalists. The Parti Nationaliste had to settle for 4 per cent of the vote.

In his throne speech in the National Assembly in October, René Lévesque confirmed his *beau risque* policy of openness to federalism. The expression *beau risque* (risk worth taking) became renowned in Quebec. But the entire episode was a sign of the great disputes that were to shake the PQ in the years that followed. Many, like Jacques Parizeau, refused to set aside their aspirations for independence and resigned. After Lévesque retired in 1985, Pierre Marc Johnson assumed the party leadership and convinced activists to put sovereignty on hold and espouse national affirmation instead. In 1988, Parizeau dislodged Johnson and once again put independence on the front burner.

Those who had opted for the *beau risque* to the point of becoming federal MPs went through the Meech Lake crisis with divided loyalties. The Accord's failure was a turning point for many MPs, the most prominent of whom was Lucien Bouchard. Bouchard resigned from the Cabinet and the Conservative caucus on May 22 1990, having denounced the tentative changes to the Meech Lake Accord.

His departure was not planned, but it was sensational. The best friend of the prime minister was leaving Cabinet in the middle of a constitutional crisis, denouncing the Charest Report, the last attempt by Brian Mulroney to save the Meech Lake Accord. Ottawa was in a state of political shock. The day seemed dark. Bouchard didn't know what to do: he saw his resignation as a failure. Dreaming of returning to his law practice, he took the road to Montreal.

1

The Member for Lac-Saint-Jean

On May 23, 1990, the ballroom in the Queen Elizabeth Hotel was full. It was a Chamber of Commerce luncheon, and 650 people, the cream of the Montreal business community, were waiting with curiosity for the speaker, who just the day before had been the federal minister of the environment. Lucien Bouchard, having just resigned from the Cabinet and the federal Conservative caucus over the Charest Report and its suggested changes to the Meech Lake Accord, faced his first audience as an independent member of Parliament. As he entered the room, a standing ovation greeted him. Wearing a blue suit, with a white flower in his buttonhole, he seemed tired until he saw the reception that awaited him.[1]

Bouchard launched into a review of the nationalist struggle, from colonization to constitutional repatriation. He lamented the divisions produced by the 1980 referendum and criticized Pierre Trudeau, Jean Chrétien, Frank McKenna, Gary Filmon and Clyde Wells. "It is a terrible thing that Quebec should be outside the constitution! People in Canada don't want to hear about that, they don't want to understand, they don't want to admit it, they don't think about it. But everything that's happening now is the result of that fact," he said, gesturing, his voice betraying his emotion.

His audience was hanging on every word.[2] He referred to Brian Mulroney's courage and the modest aims of the Meech Lake Accord, "a very important symbol that is a sign of generosity, of openness; English Canada's act of faith towards Quebec." He said, as he had before, that he had hoped to remain in the government until June 23, the deadline to approve the deal, but the content of the Charest Report and the changes it proposed to the accord had forced him out. He was not resigning with "a light heart," he said, but to be true to himself and his convictions. Denouncing the actions of Premiers

McKenna, Filmon and Wells, he urged Premier Bourassa to reject all amendments:

> The negotiations are over, the compromise has been reached, Quebec has given up everything it had. It stands naked before the nine other provinces in complete confidence, in complete honesty. Quebec has nothing more to give. But we are being asked for more. What else can we give up except our honour and what remains of our pride? Are we going to give that up? I say no, it's enough, enough, enough!

There was an almost reverent silence as he urged Quebecers to put an end to their partisan disagreements and seek a consensus among themselves to strengthen the government's position on Meech Lake. In his opinion, the political climate had never been so favourable to an examination of all the options, including sovereignty-association. "A negotiator's first duty is to create a strong bargaining position — otherwise the other side will laugh in your face. This is what is happening to us with the Meech Lake Accord," he maintained. Whatever deal is made should be placed before the public for approval through an election or a referendum, whether Meech passes or not, he said. He concluded:

> I believe in my heart that we shouldn't start anything we can't finish together. If we let ourselves become divided again, we're finished. We have to stick together. If there's a bell tolling for Quebec, it's the bell of unity, and I call on all Quebecers to join together in a great demonstration of the unity I know we can achieve.

The effect of his words was instantaneous. The ovation was even louder than when he entered the meeting. Guy Lessard, then vice-president of Provigo, expressed the mood of his colleagues. "Lucien is saying everything we believe needs to be said."[3]

Bouchard's appeal for Quebec unity produced immediate results. Two days later, Louis Laberge, president of the Quebec Federation of Labour, and Fernand Daoust, the federation's general secretary, sent a telegram to Brian Mulroney, Robert Bourassa and Lucien Bouchard.[4] Calling the Charest Report a "slap in the face" and "an insult to the intelligence of the Quebec people," Laberge and Daoust proposed that a committee made up of people from every walk of life be set up to develop a proposal for Quebec national self-affirmation in the months to come.

Bouchard was taken aback at the speed with which his message had spread and begun to take root. When he resigned, he was unsure about his future and even considered resuming his law practice. "I saw my resignation as a defeat," he says. "After battling for several months, I had failed to convince the government to leave Meech as it was . . . I didn't see what role I could play. I just wanted to save my own skin, get out of there, start living a normal life and regain some self-respect," he confided four years later. He never expected his resignation to act as the catalyst for such a groundswell of emotion.

At a press conference the previous day, Bouchard's ambivalence had led him to reject the idea of forming a pro-independence group in Parliament along with the two Conservative MPs who had resigned before him.[5] In an interview in *Le Soleil*, he said he wanted to spend the summer reflecting on the situation. The Chamber of Commerce meeting on May 23 shook his resolve, but he was still unable to say what role he planned to play in politics.[6]

The following Sunday, Bouchard was expected in his riding for a brunch that had been scheduled for a long time.[7] More than 700 people greeted him with enthusiasm, and again he gave them their money's worth. This time the target was Jean Chrétien, the next leader of the Liberal Party: "Enemy of Quebec's aspirations, ghost from 1980 come back to haunt us with his chains, scarecrow." Bouchard didn't shy away from strong language.[8] He vowed to stand in the way of Jean Chrétien and again asked Quebec to unite to accomplish this. "If English Canada isn't careful, Jean Chrétien will be the final gift, the parting gift from Quebec to English Canada," he predicted to his supporters' delight.

In the hall, Conservative party and Parti Québécois workers speculated about Bouchard's future. The conversation around the tables turned frequently to the possibility of Bouchard becoming leader of a pro-sovereignty coalition in another referendum. The wind had shifted and Bouchard realized it. Following a meeting with his constituents, he told reporters that he would continue to think over the possibilities open to him. He had ruled nothing out.[9]

In fact, he had begun to contact people he felt were key actors on the Quebec political, economic and social scene. If he looked undecided in public, he was deliberate and organized in his private determination to create a group that would reflect on the province's future.

He had already drawn up a list of people to see. The first person he contacted was Gérald Larose, president of the Confederation of National Trade Unions (CNTU). Larose was not an automatic ally. During the premiership of René Lévesque, Bouchard had been a management negotiator for the Quebec government. In 1982 he had had to implement the worst pay cuts ever imposed on public sector employees, leaving him with a reputation as "Lévesque's big stick."

Then came Claude Béland, president of the Mouvement Desjardins, QFL president Laberge and Jean Campeau, former president of the Caisse de Dépôt et de Placement. The list grew to include names such as Rita Dionne-Marsolais, later a minister in Jacques Parizeau's cabinet, Isabelle Courville, president of the PQ youth wing under former leader Pierre Marc Johnson, environmentalist Pierre Dansereau and several vice-presidents of the Caisse. Bouchard decided to see everyone he needed to in an organized fashion.

On June 6, 1990, he told journalist Michel Vastel that he was working on the creation of a formal organization and that some well-known persons were already meeting. "I've drawn up my program and I've met a lot of people," he said. [10]

The day after, on June 7, 1990, Bouchard broke ten days of silence and again basked in public adulation as he delivered another rousing speech. This time, the audience consisted of members of the Quebec Bar meeting in Pointe-au-Pic. In front of this usually reserved group, he hammered home the same message: unity, bargaining power, consensus and consultation without partisanship: "Nothing can stop us from getting what we all want! I hope Premier Bourassa remembers that we are all behind him and that, for the first time, Quebecers will stand up to support him if he comes back from the constitutional negotiations in Ottawa with his head held high."[11] He spoke without notes or a written text. He was impassioned. The audience rose to its feet, and the applause was loud and sustained. "If we need 100 per cent of the power in the areas of culture, employment and job training, we'll go and get it."

Coming on top of the Chamber of Commerce meeting and the riding brunch, the Quebec Bar meeting finally persuaded Bouchard of the need to think even more seriously about his political future. On June 12, he met with PQ leader Jacques Parizeau who, since Bouchard's resignation, had continually stated publicly that his party's doors were wide open to him. "If he is tempted," Parizeau had said immediately after Bouchard resigned, "if he wants to participate with us all in the PQ to work toward a goal he seems to share with us, he'll be welcomed with open arms."[12]

Bouchard preferred to go his own route. During the month of June, almost all the individuals he had contacted attended morning meetings in Mouvement Desjardins president Béland's conference room. They had breakfast and talked about starting a movement called Forum-Québec, aimed at studying and analysing sovereignty-related issues from a nonpartisan perspective. Bouchard had the feeling that his ideas were being translated into action.

Meanwhile, he responded to almost all requests for public appearances, called uncompromisingly for broad public consultations, and publicly weighed his plans for the future. Public forums for his ideas proliferated. On June 14, he began to write a weekly column in *Le Devoir*. On the same day, he went to the Palais des Civilisations in Montreal to attend the annual banquet of the committee in charge of organizing the annual Saint-Jean-Baptiste Day celebrations. Jacques Parizeau and Premier Bourassa were there. When Bouchard arrived, he repeated that he did not intend to stay in politics much longer and that he had only one goal: to promote the unity of Quebecers of all political allegiances. But his thinking was evolving, because he was now giving himself a year to make up his mind: "Will I sit out the rest of the parliamentary session? That will depend on what happens. I am giving myself a year to help foster a nonpartisan consensus. In a year we'll see how things have gone. That will be the time to talk about it again."[13] And the idea of a sovereignist party in federal politics? "I don't think that's an essential part of the strategy, because I believe Quebec's future will be decided in Quebec," he replied.

Bouchard knew that the Parti Québécois was campaigning for the formation of a group of independent MPs in Ottawa. He became aware of it very soon after his resignation. His telephone rang off the hook and the calls he received often had an ulterior motive. "I felt that in most cases, people had been instructed to call," he says. "There were people in the PQ who had said that [PQ vice-president Bernard] Landry and Bouchard should meet." While he resisted the idea of forming a sovereignist group, others had fewer scruples and took it upon themselves to consider it for him.

The Instability Strategy

When Bouchard resigned on May 22, many people were delighted — among them François Gérin, MP for Mégantic-Compton-Stanstead. Gérin, who had been the first of the Quebec MPs to break ranks with the Conservatives over the Charest Report, had resigned from the party on May 18, 1990. Now he felt he had found an ally. He immediately called Bouchard's resignation "a determining factor in Quebec's future" and declared that Bouchard was one of Quebec's greatest leaders. He hoped to work with Bouchard to develop a strategy for achieving sovereignty. "We are on exactly the same wavelength," Gérin continued. "In my opinion, Lucien Bouchard's resignation should encourage Premier Bourassa to maintain a very firm position" and stick to Quebec's five conditions during the constitutional talks.

Gérin had developed the idea of forming a group of MPs whose sole mission would be to defend Quebec's interests. After discussing the idea with Bernard Landry and longtime sovereignist (and Bouchard's close friend) Marc-André Bédard, Gérin became one of the key links between the PQ and the Conservative caucus before he resigned. As an independent MP, he still nurtured the idea. When Bouchard resigned, Gérin hoped that Bouchard might be used to rally disillusioned Conservatives to his project. But his hopes were frustrated by a promise Bouchard had made to Brian Mulroney. Having helped Bouchard in his byelection and having been in touch since, Gérin at first waited for a call from Bouchard. Eventually, he took the initiative. He telephoned Bouchard and asked to see him so that he could weigh the possibility of putting together a group of MPs dedicated to defending Quebec. Gérin planned to include Gilbert Chartrand, the Verdun–Saint-Paul MP who resigned on May 22, a few hours before Bouchard. "I promised Mulroney I wouldn't do any raiding," Bouchard told him. "All right, all right," Gérin answered. You could at least meet with them. There are people who want to meet with you, talk with you."

During the week, Gérin made frequent visits to Bouchard in his office. Gérin told him that "all these people will come over if someone agrees to lead the group," Bouchard recalls. Gérin was insistent and succeeded in organizing a few meetings in the minister's office that Bouchard occupied until the end of July. The first meeting was held in June. Independent MPs Bouchard, Gérin and Chartrand met with Conservatives Nic Leblanc, Benoît Tremblay, Louis Plamondon and Michel Champagne. Jacques Bouchard, the former minister's assistant, also attended. The Conservatives refused to break ranks until the fate of the Meech Lake Accord was sealed. They believed it would be pointless to form a nationalist group if the agreement passed. No one was yet talking about a sovereignist group.

Gérin did not hide his close ties with the Parti Québécois, and he exerted heavy pressure on the Conservative caucus. He repeatedly told reporters that one or another of the Conservatives was going to change sides, which put a number of Conservatives off and annoyed Bouchard. Bouchard did not want to compromise himself too deeply before Meech died or team up too quickly with the PQ. He stuck to the position that he wanted to unite all Quebecers, irrespective of their political allegiance.

No one in the PQ was worried by this. They had learned to be patient. For months they had been waiting for this moment to arrive. When he resigned, Bouchard was unaware that the operation to recruit Conservatives had begun well before Gérin had become involved. For more than a year Jacques Parizeau, PQ leader since March 1988, had headed a small group of senior PQ officials and strategists whose mission was to plan a systematic approach to the most nationalist MPs in the federal Conservative party.

The provincial election of September 25, 1989, had relegated the PQ to the opposition benches for the second time. This "contemplative life," as one of Jacques Parizeau's closest advisers put it, gave his staff time to discuss strategy. Every Monday morning in the leader's Place Ville-Marie office in Montreal, a group of five to ten people discussed how to take advantage of the cracks emerging in the federalist camp over the Meech Lake Accord. The regulars at these meetings were Parizeau, house leader Guy Chevrette, party vice-president Bernard Landry, second vice-president Paul Bégin, PQ director general Pierre Boileau and Parizeau adviser Jean Royer.

The initial goal was not to form a parliamentary group or party, but simply to induce Conservatives to leave the caucus. "The idea was to keep things in a state of controlled instability," said one insider. On the one hand, the PQ demanded that the Meech Lake Accord be passed as it was, with no amendments. On the other, they sought out Conservatives to urge them to slam the door if any changes were made or the agreement was rejected. It was a gigantic poker game based on a bet made by the PQ leader. "Parizeau predicted that if Bourassa stood his ground, the deal wouldn't pass. We staked everything on that," one adviser confides.

When it came to approaching Conservative MPs, Bernard Landry proved to be the most forward. He lived in Montreal and taught once a week at the University of Quebec in Hull. He had always been a strong advocate of a sovereignist presence in Ottawa, and he took advantage of every opportunity to woo Mulroney's MPs. He held numerous meetings in Montreal, and when he was in Hull, he invited Conservatives to eat with him at the Plaza de la Chaudière Hotel (now the Holiday Inn Crowne Plaza) or the elegant Café Henry Burger. He devoted considerable time and energy to the cause, and even kept a score sheet.

Landry wasn't the only former PQ minister who was pressed into service. Yves Duhaime, Guy Chevrette and Rodrigue Biron also took part, along with Marc-André Bédard. Jacques Parizeau himself asked Bédard to take part in the operation. Bédard had stayed in touch with a number of Conservative MPs from his home region of Saguenay–Lac-Saint-Jean. Almost all of them were former PQ activists or sympathizers; those who weren't had at least voted Yes in the 1980 referendum.

Because he had kept his ties with these MPs, Bédard had a good idea of what the atmosphere was like in Mulroney's Quebec caucus, and Parizeau knew it. He wanted to be kept informed. Since Bédard held no official party post, he inspired more trust than someone like Bernard Landry. Bédard also understood Parizeau's view of the situation and sympathized with it. "If Meech failed, it was essential that there be a series of resignations or at least one key resignation," he recalls. He agreed to do his part.

The small Monday morning group didn't stop there. It also called on party workers to inquire into Conservatives' state of mind. For example, a lawyer who knew Tory minister Pierre Blais well was asked to find out whether there was any chance of his resigning. The answer was No, so no approach was attempted. In other cases, a meeting was actually set up with the leader to help tip the balance.

But the Monday morning group relied most heavily on the ties formed through the period of the *beau risque*, when the PQ had decided to support the Conservatives in the 1984 and 1988 general elections. "For many, contacting MPs was not very complicated. It was almost natural. It was a matter of finding someone who knew a particular MP well enough to try to convince him to resign," explains one of Parizeau's close associates. Sometimes the pressure was put on if "someone in their inner circle told us that it was worth testing" the MP, he adds. Marc-André Bédard was in the most sensitive position at the time because of his friendship with Lucien Bouchard, who was at the time Mulroney's Quebec lieutenant. Bédard refrained from telling Bouchard what was going on and refused to extract information from him. It was a matter of protecting a longstanding relationship and shielding a true friend from embarrassment.

This operation required considerable effort. More than thirty Conservatives were approached, including ministers like Benoît Bouchard, Gilles Loiselle and Monique Vézina. Parizeau's advisers had to admit that the results were mixed. Some MPs slipped through their fingers at the last minute. This is what happened with Jean-Marc Robitaille, MP for Terrebonne, who even telephoned Parizeau to tell him he was resigning. He said he would make his announcement at a meeting of the Quebec caucus in Gaspé. He never followed through. Shortly afterwards, he was appointed a parliamentary secretary. Bouchard's resignation made up for the small number of recruits. It was not just a consolation prize — it was a real gift. Bouchard had style and charisma; he was respected and credible; he knew how to reach out to people. He was the man of the hour.

"Gérin was one of the first to push for the idea of a group in Ottawa," recalls a PQ adviser. "But we said what we needed was a leader." At first, hopes were placed on Benoît Bouchard, and then on Gilles Loiselle and Monique Vézina. But nothing happened; these ministers, whose nationalist convictions were well known, hung on. Lucien Bouchard was also a well-known nationalist, but no one in the PQ dared approach him. "We felt that Bouchard's loyalty to Mulroney was such that he would not let himself even give the impression that he was dissatisfied with the decisions being made," notes the adviser. But the resignation of Bouchard, admits Landry, "was our secret hope."

The impact of his resignation and the public response to it quickly made him the unexpected but longed-for leader. However, his resignation had an unforeseen effect. It whipped up the Mulroney loyalists, who went all out to ward off further defections, notes one PQ organizer. Thus, when the Meech Lake Accord foundered in the Manitoba and Newfoundland legislatures, only a few of the resignations the PQ had hoped for actually occurred.

A Strange Combination

It was an emotional time. The public was able to follow the Meech Lake drama live on television as it unfolded simultaneously in Newfoundland, Manitoba and Calgary, where the federal Liberal leadership convention was taking place. When the Accord's failure was confirmed on the evening of June 22, there was tumult. In Quebec City, Premier Robert Bourassa seized the public imagination with his famous statement: "No matter what anyone says or does, Quebec has always been, is now and will always be a distinct society, free and capable of taking responsibility for its destiny and development."

The next day in Calgary, Jean Lapierre, MP for Shefford, and Gilles Rocheleau, MP for Hull-Aylmer, dramatically walked out of the Liberal convention, declaring that they were unable to serve under their new leader, Jean Chrétien — in their view one of the people responsible for the failure of Meech.

Gérin lost no time in immediately telephoning his friend Louis Plamondon, Conservative MP for Richelieu. Montreal's Saint-Jean-Baptiste Day parade, the first since 1969, was scheduled for Sunday, June 24. He wanted to make something happen for the occasion and knew that Plamondon was only waiting for the right moment to free himself from the weight he had been carrying around for months. "I had told Gérin I would see it through, that I would take it as far as I could. I did that, I hung on to the end," Plamondon confides.

But the conclusion of a new agreement accompanied by a parallel resolution in early June left him totally dissatisfied: "I was really disappointed, I really hesitated. I almost resigned the following Monday." But he stayed because he had promised he would. In the end, the Accord's failure felt like a kind of deliverance to him: "I felt liberated when it fell apart. I felt that my decision would be an easy one to make. If it had passed, I could have lived with it, but I think I always would have wondered whether, as a sovereignist who had always believed in Quebec, I had lacked courage."

Gérin also received a call from the MP for Rosemont, Benoît Tremblay, who told him that he had made up his mind. He would march in the parade and intended to resign. In fact, his mind had been made up for a long time. Since February, Tremblay had no longer supported Mulroney's "parallel tracks" approach to the Meech Lake Accord. Tremblay was a former assistant deputy minister of industry and commerce under the PQ government and considered the agreement a strict minimum. To settle for less was unacceptable. A man who planned ahead, he set headhunters to work on finding him alternative employment and remained silent. First elected in 1988, he was not entitled to a pension, and he did not want to resign without another job to go to. He also had another reason for waiting: he hoped that if they chose the right moment, he and his colleagues could set off a larger chain reaction.

Gérin told Bouchard that several Conservatives were thinking of resigning and wanted to march beside him in the Saint-Jean-Baptiste Day parade, delayed one day because of the rain. They agreed to meet at the corner of Hôtel-de-Ville and Sherbrooke streets. Treasury Board President Gilles Loiselle, invited by Bouchard, almost joined them. He went to the designated meeting place, but he hesitated when he realized the impact his presence would have. Reconsidering, he turned and left.

The parade was impressive. Between 200,000 and 300,000 people took part. The atmosphere was calm, and Sherbrooke Street was transformed into a river of blue and white fleurs-de-lys. As Gilles Loiselle had feared, the presence of Conservative MPs drew the television cameras. Plamondon was not surprised. He refused to announce his resignation to questioning reporters. He wanted to do it in the House of Commons. He simply repeated that "if [Quebec] isn't a distinct society, it will be a distinct country." Brian Mulroney's new Quebec lieutenant, Benoît Bouchard, was startled when he saw the MPs on television. He grabbed the telephone and left messages for them, intending to try to persuade them not to break ranks.

A message from Mulroney was awaiting Plamondon at home. Tremblay went to his nephew's birthday party after the parade, and when he got home around midnight, he found fourteen messages on his answering machine from Mulroney and Benoît Bouchard, saying they wanted to talk to him. He returned Bouchard's call. The conversation was brief and left him unmoved. He then telephoned Mulroney. This conversation was very onesided and lasted an hour and a half. It didn't shake him, but he was surprised at how long it went on. "I understand why others stayed," says Tremblay. "It showed [Mulroney] was determined, and that's probably why many others didn't resign."

The following Tuesday three Conservatives and one Liberal announced in the House of Commons that they would henceforth sit as independents. "No more compromises that would be even more humiliating! My pride and dignity need time to heal, and from now on, I want to devote my energies only to Quebec," stated Louis Plamondon. "I will never accept the legacy of Lord Durham," he concluded. "I have decided to fully support the nonpartisan movement launched by the honourable member for Lac-Saint-Jean," said Benoît Tremblay. The third Conservative to resign was Nic Leblanc, MP for Longueuil since 1984. This reserved man reiterated what his colleagues had said. He congratulated Brian Mulroney for his courage and expressed regret that he could no longer follow the prime minister's leadership. "To those who think that some day they will govern Canada on the basis of an obsolete vision of this country, I say that Quebec's motto is: *Je me souviens*," he warned.[14]

Liberal Jean Lapierre did not mince words. Attacking the Liberal opponents of the Meech Lake Accord, he reminded them that the commitment to a renewed federalism made by Pierre Elliott Trudeau on May 15, 1980 at the Paul Sauvé Arena had not been upheld. "I feel sad, humiliated and betrayed," he said. "For those who thought that Meech was too much, take note that from now on it is not enough."[15]

Lapierre, who had been an MP since 1979, waited until mid-July before publicly joining the group of Conservatives. But he knew how to make himself wanted, while making his own approaches. His decision to resign from the Liberal Party had been made a long time before. Having no intention of serving under Jean Chrétien, he had contacted the Conservatives early on. In May, even before Gérin resigned, the two MPs met over a meal in Magog. Gérin told him he wanted to break ranks. Lapierre told Gérin about his discovery of the history of the Bloc Populaire, the party established during World War II in reaction to the Conscription Crisis. What he had in mind was to set up an informal parliamentary group whose purpose was to uphold Quebec's interests. Lapierre maintains that Gérin took the first step. Gérin claims it was Lapierre. But the two agree on the account of their conversation.

Lapierre also saw Plamondon. In late May, Lapierre told Plamondon he wanted to leave and do it with the largest possible impact. However, he did not want to act on his own and risk wasting the gesture. Once he was going to do something dramatic, he wanted to make sure it would resonate for as long as possible. For him, this meant forming a nonpartisan parliamentary group with a leader who would have some effect. He already had his eye on Bouchard.

A few days before leaving for the Liberal leadership convention in Calgary, Lapierre went to see Bouchard. Bouchard was packing because, as an independent, he was being forced to move to a new office. "I'm leaving. I'm on my way to the Calgary convention in a week. I think we've had it. I think it's all over for Meech," Lapierre told Bouchard. Lapierre wanted to prevent the newly independent MPs from resigning their seats. "If we open up our ridings, for God's sake, Chrétien will become leader of the Liberal party and he'll win our ridings and we'll look really stupid," he continued. He told Bouchard about his discovery of the history of the Bloc Populaire and his desire to form a parliamentary group committed to Quebec's interests. On that note, he left for Calgary.

When Lapierre came back, Bouchard was one of the first people he approached. "Lapierre said to me, we'll get together ... and then, Rocheleau might be there too but that will be harder: he is not very sovereignist yet," Bouchard recounts. Even though he kept his distance publicly, Lapierre was active behind the scenes, Bouchard revealed on June 27.[16] "I have spoken to MP Jean Lapierre and we are planning to develop a strategy," he told the press as he came out of a meeting with 400 members of the Sainte-Foy Chamber of Commerce.

A Time for Action

When Lapierre delayed publicly joining the former Conservatives, they decided not to wait any longer. On June 29, the ex-Conservatives all met at Nic Leblanc's riding office in Longueuil. The meeting dragged on, lasting almost five hours.[17] When they emerged, the MPs confirmed Bouchard as their leader and declared that they would support the Conservatives whenever their actions corresponded to Quebec's interests.

But their main concern was the byelection in Laurier–Sainte-Marie, which had been called for August 13. The seat had been vacant since Liberal Jean-Claude Malépart's death from cancer. The six MPs had not yet decided whether to participate in the election, even though, as Bouchard admitted, a number of people had said they were interested. Bouchard's indecisiveness was surprising because, two days before, he had challenged new Liberal leader Jean Chrétien to run in Laurier–Sainte-Marie against an independent sovereignist.[18] Running a candidate in the byelection would maintain momentum in favour of sovereignty throughout the summer and help the credibility of Bouchard's group.

The ex-Conservatives were not alone in setting their sights on Laurier–Sainte-Marie. In fact, they were perhaps the last ones to do so. Once again, the PQ had thought of it before they did. Just six days after Bouchard's resignation, PQ pollster Michel Lepage conducted an opinion poll in Laurier–Sainte-Marie. How would a sovereignist perform in the byelection? However the question was worded, Lepage found that a sovereignist candidate would win handily. But the poll, conducted from May 28 to June 1, also showed that a candidate would do best if he or she were the choice of Lucien

Bouchard. The PQ was delighted, and looked for ways to persuade Bouchard to throw himself into the battle.

Before Meech's death, Bouchard had agreed to a private dinner with Jacques Parizeau at the PQ leader's home in the Montreal suburb of Outremont. Over dessert, Parizeau handed him Lepage's poll. The handwritten information was an eye-opener. It promised a Bouchard candidate more than 66 per cent of the vote. "It was a landslide. I could see it was for real and I gave the okay," Bouchard recalls. The group of MPs, who learned of the poll at the meeting in Nic Leblanc's office, agreed, despite some doubts, to have Bouchard choose the candidate. So he launched a search.

During the next few days, Bouchard approached several people. Some declined, dissuaded by their associates. Others were unsuitable. On the suggestion of the PQ, he finally chose a former PQ MNA, Denise Leblanc-Bantey. But the other independent MPs and some of his advisers objected. They had nothing against Leblanc-Bantey, an experienced parliamentarian, but they felt a new group whose goal was to bring people together should project a new image. The ideal candidate should not be so obviously associated with one of the traditional parties. Bouchard, placed in an awkward position, reluctantly withdrew his selection.

Then, on July 5, Benoît Tremblay's assistant received a call from trade union negotiator Gilles Duceppe. Duceppe, the son of the popular actor Jean Duceppe, had been thinking of entering politics for some time. Duceppe had already tested the idea of running as a candidate in Laurier–Sainte-Marie on a number of old friends, including Pierre-Paul Roy and Montreal Mayor Jean Doré. Duceppe wanted to approach Bouchard, but he didn't know whether Bouchard had found a candidate. He took a chance and informed Tremblay's assistant, whom he knew, that he was interested. When Tremblay learned about it, he called Duceppe back the same day and told him to see Bouchard. He had to do this soon because a public meeting was scheduled for July 11, and the election date was fast approaching. On July 6, Duceppe met with Bouchard, who had set up his Montreal headquarters in the Queen Elizabeth Hotel. Bouchard's wife, Audrey, was there along with their son Alexandre, who was in diapers and babbled at visitors.

Duceppe, who was overseeing a major round of negotiations in the hotel industry, was exhausted. He hadn't slept in sixty hours. "He looked terrible. He's usually nervous anyway. He was wired," Bouchard recalls. But the two negotiators managed to "connect."

Bouchard, a former establishment lawyer, was seriously considering choosing Duceppe, a former Maoist, as candidate. Bouchard's staff was delighted. Duceppe was just the right person. He came across well, he was new to politics and, to top it all off, he was Jean Duceppe's son. A few days earlier, Jean Duceppe had brought the crowd to its feet with his Saint-Jean-Baptiste Day parade closing speech.

On July 8, Bouchard told Duceppe he needed him. But Duceppe couldn't let the striking workers down at such a critical point. Bouchard called CNTU president Gérald Larose to try to find a solution, but there was nothing to be done. Luck, however, was on Bouchard's side. On July 9, a tentative agreement was reached in the hotel negotiations. Duceppe was finally free.

While Duceppe was in negotiations, Bouchard worried. What about the organizational aspect? Marc-André Bédard told him to speak to Louise Harel, PQ MNA for Maisonneuve and longtime acquaintance of Duceppe's. She had doubts about the venture but nonetheless directed Bouchard to the local organizer — Yves "Bob" Dufour. Dufour was a former docker, union and student activist, and PQ organizer before deciding in 1973 to return to the land. After three years near Trois-Pistoles, he returned to Montreal at the request of Louise Harel. He worked for the PQ MNA Guy Bisaillon before joining Guy Chevrette's ministerial staff in Montreal. Defeated as a PQ candidate in Sainte-Marie in 1985, Dufour retired from politics, bought shares in a brasserie on Ontario Street in the east end of Montreal and worked with young people who were mentally handicapped.

Bouchard called Dufour, and they agreed to meet that very evening at his Ontario Street brasserie. For the first time in his life, the MP from Lac-Saint-Jean set foot in east-end Montreal, one of the city's poorest districts. The bar was dark. "It was hot in there, and was full of sinister-looking guys with large beers. Someone was wiping up behind the bar," recounts Bouchard, describing the scene and imitating the people he saw.

"Is Bob Dufour here?"

"Bob!" the man shouted. "There's someone here to see you. Bob!"

"There I was in my suit and tie," Bouchard continues. "This guy came out from the back of the room. It was a big, long room. He was at the back and moved forward into the light. I couldn't see anything and then, there he was. He's a big guy. And he comes across as a loudmouth when you don't know him."

"What do you want?" Dufour asked.

"I'd like to chat with you," Bouchard answered.

"What about?"

"Um — politics."

"What do you mean, politics? What kind of politics?" He was so obnoxious it could make someone want to turn around and walk out. But he finally said, "Sit down, let's have a beer."

The two men sat down together with Benoît Tremblay, who was accompanying Bouchard, in front of few large beers. Dufour listened as Bouchard told him that he was looking for a candidate for the byelection. Dufour complained that the whole idea was unrealistic. He was sure nothing could be done because there were only four weeks left in the campaign and the organizers who were still available were away on holiday. "It won't work, you'll get wiped out. You have no organization, no program, no money, no candidate. You're a leader of nothing and you're going to get crushed," Dufour told Bouchard to his face.

Dufour, who had already refused the PQ executive director's offer to be the organizer unless Duceppe was the candidate, was determined to test Bouchard. He didn't tell him right away that many organizers from provincial ridings that overlapped with Laurier–Sainte-Marie were prepared to help. Dufour had considerable election experience and wanted to know if Bouchard knew what he was up against. Dufour asked him to predict what was going to happen. "If you want the Liberals to get in, keep on talking like that, for Chrissake," said Bouchard angrily. Dufour was surprised to hear the other man swear and asked him why he thought the Liberals were running second in the riding. Bouchard said he had heard it from the PQ's pollster. The discussion became more serious. Dufour began to listen more attentively and to criticize the Liberals.

Gilles Duceppe's candidacy was the only thing that would bring Dufour on board. Bouchard thought as much, because he knew they were friends. However, he didn't know they had known each other for more than twenty years, since they had been activists together in Montreal student movements. Dufour finally decided to join the campaign and did so with so much conviction that he became one of the party's most faithful organizers.

Duceppe had barely forty-eight hours to rest up. The public meeting at which Bouchard was to introduce him was scheduled for July 11, in the basement of Saint-Louis-de-Gonzague Church. It was Gérin who had persuaded the group to schedule a meeting and organize it without knowing who the candidate would be. The important thing was to be ready on time. Gérin got in touch with the Saint-Louis brothers, a family well known in PQ circles and to Bob Dufour. They and the group they belonged to, the Mouvement Souverainiste du Québec, made the evening a success. More than 800 people attended, including PQ MNAs André Boulerice and Michel Bourdon, CNTU president Gérald Larose and pro-independence activist Doris Lussier. Liberal MNA Jacques Chagnon sent the new candidate a good luck message.

Bouchard's small group launched its campaign with no resources. In the early days, the small campaign staff called the troops from a small table in Dufour's Ontario Street brasserie, using the establishment's public telephone. A few young Liberals and one of Jean Lapierre's assistants joined the campaign, but most of the organizers came from the PQ ranks. On the communications staff was a full-time PQ official, François Leblanc. Pierre-Paul Roy and Dufour worked nonstop and managed to recruit 225 people to get the vote out between 4 and 8 P.M. on election day.

The campaign went without a hitch. Momentum was with Duceppe, and luck as well. A few days before the election, Liberal candidate Denis Coderre declared on television that he was the spiritual son of the late Jean-Claude Malépart, a populist and defender of the poor who had been well liked by his constituents. Malépart's widow was furious. She repudiated Coderre and came out in favour of Duceppe. It was a final, unexpected boost. Jean Lapierre officially joined Bouchard's group during the campaign. This was when the MPs adopted a "mission" and a name that took hold in the media: Bloc Québécois.

On August 13, for the first time in Canadian history, an openly sovereignist Quebec MP was elected to the House of Commons. Gilles Duceppe won almost 67 per cent of the vote. It was a heady time. The Bloc's candidate had won, Bouchard was preparing to participate in one of the largest Quebec constitutional consultations ever to be held, the parliamentary session would begin soon, and the polls were favourable. The Bloc had the wind in its sails.

2

The Birth of the Bloc

The man behind the Bloc's success was a late bloomer in politics. Lucien Bouchard is a prudent man, one who still perceives himself primarily as a lawyer. Born on December 22, 1939 in the parish of Saint-Coeur-de-Marie in Lac-Saint-Jean, Bouchard comes from a humble background. His father, a trucker who could scarcely read and write and whom Bouchard has admired all his life, succeeded through much sacrifice to send his four sons to a boys' seminary and then to university.

Lucien, the eldest, set foot in Quebec City for the first time at age fourteen; six years later he returned to study social sciences at Laval University. He completed his baccalaureate in a year and then decided on law. His roommate throughout these years was André Tremblay, who went on to become Bourassa's adviser. In the faculty classrooms, Bouchard rubbed shoulders with future political notables such as Brian Mulroney, Pierre de Bané, André Ouellet, Jean Garon, Michael Meighen and Peter White. He edited the student newspaper, *Le Carabin*, with future PQ minister Denis de Belleval. Timid, studious, a lover of literature, he became close friends with Mulroney near the end of his studies.

Unlike his friends, Bouchard did not set up practice in the big city when he graduated in 1964, but instead returned to Chicoutimi. After a few years in the background, he found himself negotiating the transfer of private institutions — the Chicoutimi hospital and seminary — to the public sector. Then, in 1970, at thirty-one, he became the first chair of the education arbitration tribunals, where he met the future PQ minister Guy Chevrette, Jean-Roch Boivin who would become René Lévesque's chief of staff, and a former professor, Robert Cliche. He kept this post until 1976.

During this period, along with the majority of Quebecers, Bouchard supported Pierre Trudeau. In 1968, he campaigned to get Trudeau elected. For a brief period, he was even vice-president of the policy commission of the federal Liberal party's Quebec wing.

In 1970, he joined Robert Bourassa's Liberals. But the October Crisis and the altercations between the two Liberal first ministers undermined his federalist beliefs and persuaded him of the virtues of nationalism as incarnated in René Lévesque.

At the invitation of a friend, Marc-André Bédard, Bouchard eventually agreed to join the Parti Québécois. He became a card-carrying member in 1971 or 1972 when Jacques Parizeau was passing through the area. After actively campaigning for his PQ friend in 1973, however, his comfortable universe crumbled. His Liberal law partners did not appreciate Bouchard's activism and demanded that their contract be altered to prevent it. Bouchard refused and quit. He had to rebuild a new clientele from scratch.

When his fortunes were at their lowest, Robert Cliche, Guy Chevrette and Brian Mulroney, of the newly named Cliche Commission inquiring into the construction industry, gave him a new lease on life as commission prosecutor. For a year, he led the charge against corruption in the industry amid a great deal of media attention.

As a well-established lawyer, he worked for several years on various committees of the Quebec Bar. Contrary to popular belief, Bouchard was not a small-scale provincial lawyer. He became, as he says himself, an establishment lawyer, and despite his PQ allegiances, he received special mandates from the Quebec Liberal government to negotiate with employees in the health sector.

He maintained his contacts in the Parti Québécois. But, despite his admiration for René Lévesque, Bouchard nonetheless refused Lévesque's invitation to run for office under the PQ banner in the 1976 election. He also turned down an offer to become deputy minister of labour. It was finally Yves Martin who recruited him to sit on the commission charged with reviewing the negotiating framework in the public and parapublic sectors. Indeed, the conclusions these two men wrote up were known as the Martin-Bouchard Report.

In 1978, Jean-Roch Boivin approached him, at Lévesque's request, to be the government's chief negotiator in a round of talks with Quebec's public servants. Bouchard reached an agreement that seemed to guarantee social peace on the eve of the 1980 referendum. But a year later, the province's financial crisis forced the government to withdraw the increase promised for the start of 1982. The drastic reduction in employees' salaries was taken as an affront. Bouchard, still acting as state negotiator, insisted that his honorarium be cut as well. Despite his efforts, he was caricatured in a collective dramatic work commissioned by the unions and presented at the Théâtre Parminou. It was entitled "Happy Crisis Lucien!"

During this period, he was one of the Quebec government lawyers contesting Pierre Elliott Trudeau's unilateral repatriation of the constitution at the Supreme Court of Canada. He was also the government's prosecutor when Quebec charged Newfoundland with breaking its contract regarding the supply of electricity from Churchill Falls.

In 1982, after his tribulations with the public service, Bouchard returned to Chicoutimi and turned down his friend Pierre Marc Johnson's offer to become deputy minister of justice. Still, over the years, he did agree to sit on the boards of directors of the General Investment Corporation, Donohue Forestry and the Canadian Development Investment Corporation.

Then, in 1983, his friend Brian Mulroney (from whom he had distanced himself during the referendum) was elected to the leadership of the Conservative party. Bouchard agreed to give him a hand, write his speeches. He encouraged a softening of Mulroney's position with regard to Quebec and worked for him during the 1984 election campaign. Although he was one of Brian Mulroney's first political advisers, Bouchard recoiled when he was asked to become a candidate himself.

"I have always refused to get into politics, he recalls. I have always said No — No to the Liberals, to Lévesque a number of times, to Mulroney. I have said No because, consciously and with lucidity, I didn't want to do politics ... I knew it was the way to change things. But I have always refused to go." He had a feeling he didn't have what it took to make it in the political arena. "I was afraid of politics. In fact, I was afraid to fail. And at the same time, I was successful in my law career and I was making money. It is not easy to quit a job where you're making money and choose the insecurity of politics."

By offering him the Canadian ambassadorship in Paris, Mulroney found another means to make his friend part of the Tory machine. Bouchard, a lover of letters and history, could not turn down the opportunity to live in the city of lights. His nomination in August 1985 was instantly attacked in English Canada where his loyalty was questioned. After years of wrangling, he succeeded in normalizing relations between Paris and Ottawa, which enabled the launch of the Francophonie, the Commonwealth equivalent for Francophone countries. He was later recognized as one of the principal architects of the first three Francophone summits in Paris, Quebec City and Dakar.[1] But the distrust manifested by the English press marked him. When he resigned, he confided that he had "underestimated the intensity of the paranoia — separatists are worse than the mafia to English Canada."[2]

In 1988, Bouchard could resist the call to politics no longer. This time, it was at the invitation of his best friend, to whom he owed several favours. With the integrity of the government under constant attack and suffering in the polls, Mulroney needed new blood and Bouchard quickly became the long-awaited Mr. Clean. Bouchard joined the Cabinet on March 31, 1988 as Secretary of State, although he was only elected to Parliament two months later in a June byelection in Lac-Saint-Jean. In 1989, he became environment minister and immediately put more than one back up when he announced that all government decisions would in the future have to be submitted for environmental evaluation.

His appointment to the Cabinet created ripples. He was not one to be muzzled and generally spoke his mind. More than once, this embarrassed Mulroney, who nevertheless continued to support him. When Quebec used the notwithstanding clause in the Constitution to adopt Bill 178 limiting signs in languages other than French at the end of 1988, Bouchard supported Bourassa. Even though the law did not please him, he recognized that the province had the constitutional right to make use of this clause. Mulroney, who disapproved of the very existence of the notwithstanding clause, refused to reprimand his minister publicly. Nor did he do so when Bouchard argued, after Clyde Wells rescinded his legislature's support of the Meech Accord, that Canada should choose between Newfoundland and Quebec.

But the Charest Report finally forced a break. As Bouchard wrote in his letter of resignation, he knew that his gesture "had wounded an old and tried friendship." But, he added, for him it was a question of principle and he could not retreat. While complimenting his friend, he nevertheless recognized their differences regarding the country's future. "I am all the more pained at what has separated us in that I have great admiration for the courage and lucidity with which you have undertaken the work of reconciliation."

The separation was extremely painful and Mulroney, according to those close to him, still bears a grudge against the man whom his biographer, Ian MacDonald, described as "the only one who could see into Mulroney's soul."[3] In Mulroney's entourage, Bouchard's resignation was referred to as the coup mounted to ensure the death of Meech Lake.[4]

The resignation isolated Bouchard from many among his circle of acquaintances and friends. Unlike the leaders of the traditional parties, he became a leader without long-time friends at his side. He found himself surrounded by strangers and even former union and political adversaries. To this day, there is no one in his greatly reduced entourage who knew him personally before 1990. Pierre-Paul Roy, who became his first chief of staff, admitted he was surprised to discover on his arrival what a solitary man Bouchard was, despite being the most popular politician in Quebec. He used the public transit system, faced a divided caucus each day and had no staff. "He was alone most of the time," explained Roy.

From the Back Benches to Centre Stage

When Meech died, Jacques Parizeau adopted a conciliatory policy, stating that he favoured holding an *États généraux* to bring together all sectors of Quebec society, including the federal MPs.[5] The Liberal government had rejected such a suggestion earlier, in April, but by June the situation was different. The rejection of the constitutional accord had resulted in a wave of support for sovereignty stronger than ever before.[6] Robert Bourassa, known for hedging his bets and for his dislike of precipitous action, understood that he would have to manage this new situation. He would have to play for time. Under the circumstances, Parizeau's suggestion was too good to be rejected. It simply needed a few changes.

On June 29, 1990 Bourassa and Parizeau agreed to create an enlarged parliamentary commission to study Quebec's political and constitutional future, the Bélanger-Campeau Commission. On July 2, Bourassa called Lucien Bouchard and invited him to a meeting at the Bunker, his office in Quebec City. Bouchard had a good idea of what they would discuss before he arrived.

Bouchard was pleased at the prospect of a Commission seat. Since his resignation in May, he had called upon Quebecers to unite, in any way possible, to develop a common position that could later be submitted to the population through a referendum or an election. But Bouchard's suggestions had nothing to do with Bourassa's reasons for inviting him to sit on the Commission.

Bourassa always evaluated a situation according to the room it gave him to manoeuvre. When Bouchard resigned, Bourassa sympathized with Mulroney: the resignation created complications for the prime minister. But from Quebec's perspective, Bouchard's gesture made clear to English Canada that the death of Meech would not be without consequences.

With the Accord rejected, creating a commission without giving a place to Bouchard would be difficult. "It seemed obvious that if [the federal Liberals] and [the Conservatives] were to be present as representatives of the Commons, it would have been quite illogical to exclude Lucien Bouchard," remembers a close associate of Bourassa. "In the context, Bouchard's presence could not be avoided."

The men had seen each other a few days earlier at a Saint-Jean-Baptiste banquet at Montreal's Palais de la Civilisation. As they exchanged a solid handshake, Bourassa remarked to Bouchard, "Your friend in Ottawa misses you." Bouchard was touched. Their meeting on the roof of the Bunker had the same relaxed and friendly tone. The conversation was human and personal, and Bouchard found Bourassa sympathetic and kind. Bourassa even offered to give the Bloc leader the results of a poll conducted in Laurier–Saint-Marie.

The premier stressed the importance of showing solidarity among Quebecers. In his opinion, Bouchard could play a useful role on the Commission when the time came to examine the various possible options. "He let me understand that, politically, things could be accomplished," says the Bloc leader. "What exactly? He didn't say."

Bouchard was the first person to be offered a seat on the Bélanger-Campeau Commission. Flattered, he accepted immediately, but made no commitments in favour of one option or another. Bourassa, for his part, posed no conditions. This would be their only private meeting. Nonetheless, for Bouchard it was a gift from the gods. After resigning and being relegated to the farthest back benches of the House of Commons, he now found himself at centre-stage in one of the most important constitutional consultations ever undertaken in Quebec.

The Commission was an opportunity to show his skills, refine his positions and, above all, make new links and strengthen old ones. The Commission would also become the new platform for most members of Forum-Québec. Almost all would sit on the Commission, forming what became known as the "nonaligned" group. Bouchard still smiles when he thinks of it. "Perhaps Bourassa didn't realize this, but it was almost a miracle. The Bélanger-Campeau Commission was a bigger, better Forum-Québec, financed by the state."

Bouchard became the natural leader of the nonaligned group of sovereignists on the Commission. Alongside Bouchard were the union leaders — the CNTU's Gérald Larose, the QFL's Louis Laberge, and the CEQ's Lorraine Pagé — as well as Claude Béland, president of the Mouvement Desjardins, Jacques Proulx, president of the Union des Producteurs Agricoles, Serge Turgeon, president of the Union des Artistes, Roger Nicolet, president of the Union des Municipalités Régionales de Comté and, lastly, Jean-Claude Beaumier, representing the Union des Municipalités du Québec.

But the consensus within this nonaligned group was a problem for the sovereignist side, since it led to a division along PQ and non-PQ lines. The two groups disagreed on two things: the inclusion of two possible future hypotheses in the final report, either sovereignty or acceptable federal offers, and the commission's recommendation concerning the date of the referendum on sovereignty.

This division among the sovereignists was not unwelcome to Bourassa, who was extremely pleased to have named Bouchard, leader of the nonaligned, to the Commission. "He had not contributed to sovereignist unity," says a source close to the premier. "Given the context, although he might not have expected the result, [Bourassa] could not regret his decision, since it had caused serious problems for the PQ."

"Lucien worked very hard, and he was constantly in conflict with Parizeau and the PQ hardliners," remembers Jean-Claude Rivest, Bourassa's long-time adviser.

Duet for Obstinate Voices

Whatever Bourassa's reasons for appointing Bouchard, it was a sign of encouragement for the little group of independent MPs. Two other members of the group — Jean Lapierre and Gilles Rocheleau — also received encouragement from the premier. As Lapierre and Rocheleau tried to decide their political futures that summer, Bourassa seemed to nudge them gently in the direction of Bouchard.

Lapierre was young and intelligent, with significant parliamentary experience; a politician skilled at playing his cards right. In 1974, aged only eighteen, he was named a special assistant to André Ouellet, then minister of consumer and corporate affairs. In 1976, he became chief of staff of the minister of state for urban affairs. He was only twenty-three when he was elected federal member of Parliament for Shefford in 1979. Lapierre campaigned actively for the No side in the referendum and voted for the repatriation of the constitution in 1982. A John Turner supporter, at age twenty-eight he became one of the youngest Cabinet ministers in Canadian history when named minister of state for amateur sport.

Once in opposition, John Turner made him critic for constitutional affairs, but following the Meech Lake Accord, Lapierre soon found himself facing firm resistance from many of his colleagues. He supported Turner in his defence of Meech Lake, but after Turner left as Liberal leader, the other side felt that they had a free hand. A break between Lapierre and the Liberal party seemed inevitable.

"For me," Lapierre said at the time, "Meech Lake seemed to promise at least some kind of renewed federalism. I said to myself, if we can't even deliver on this, I'm going home. I have other things to do. I've wasted enough time in politics."

As co-chair of Paul Martin's Liberal leadership campaign, Lapierre took advantage of his travels around the country to defend the constitutional accord, but as the months went by pessimism set in. He felt betrayed by his Liberal colleagues, and was increasingly isolated in caucus. "I had the feeling that everyone was forgetting our promises," he says. "My colleagues and I had made commitments to Quebecers, and now those same people were doing everything in their power to sink Meech."

In the spring of 1990, he had attended a cocktail party hosted by his friend Jacques Bouchard, publisher of the Granby newspaper *La Voix de l'Est*. As a good Liberal, Lapierre was dubious about former Péquiste Lucien Bouchard. The publisher of *La Voix de l'Est* painted a sympathetic picture of Bouchard, however, and recommended that the two MPs meet. And so, Lapierre approached Bouchard before going to the Liberal leadership convention in Calgary and again after he had returned.

When Lapierre went home that summer to the Magdalen Islands, he invited a number of former Tories to join him. François Gérin and Benoît Tremblay accepted the invitation and spent a few days with Lapierre at his cottage. The three men discussed the group that had been formed at the meeting in Nic Leblanc's office on June 29. Lapierre avoided any formal commitments, however. He did not want to find himself either controlled by the former Tories or used by the PQ. Above all, he was still a Liberal. He might have burned his bridges with the federal party, but there was no question of doing the same thing with the Quebec Liberals. He had been a member of the Quebec party since he was a teenager. All his best friends were members. He had taken part in every election campaign and had been very active in the youth wing.

After Gérin and Tremblay's visit to his cottage, Lapierre took the initiative. He began working on a document to define what he saw as the role of the Bloc. He contacted Bouchard again, and the two began to work on the text together.

"He arrived with parts already written," Bouchard remembers. "I know the Liberals, and what he had was Liberal writing. They talk about sovereignty, but not seriously. They skate around the question, talk about autonomy." He insisted that Lapierre make clear references to sovereignty. Lapierre agreed, but it was not easy. "He had added the word sovereignty all through the mission statement, and that was difficult for me. The word stuck in my throat," Lapierre remembers.

As they worked together on the text, the chemistry was good. Bouchard asked Lapierre's opinion on the byelection in Laurier–Sainte-Marie. Covering himself as usual, Lapierre did not make a commitment, but the two men got along.

Lapierre was determined to protect his independence, and he put his cards on the table. "Lucien," he said, "we can never have the same agenda; we don't have the same political background. I'll never accept being pulled along by your coattails [but] if we can do something together ... if we can help create a political force, well, perhaps we can accomplish something together."

Their mutual confidence grew. This was essential for the young Liberal MP, since for Lapierre the party was the leader; it was the leader that you had to work with. "I never talked to the others because Lucien was their leader," Lapierre remarks. But Lapierre also had another leader: Bourassa. Upon his return to Montreal, Lapierre sent a copy of the finished document, not just to Bouchard, but also to his friend, Jean-Claude Rivest, one of the Quebec premier's chief advisers. Lapierre knew that Bourassa would have heard what was going on and, since he wanted to meet with the premier, thought it better to keep him informed.

On July 10, Bourassa and Lapierre met at the Bunker. Lapierre gave his piece about the Bloc Populaire, about building a favourable balance of forces. He brought up the Bélanger-Campeau Commission. "Understand," he said to Bourassa, "I have a choice. Either I pack up and go home, or I stick around in Ottawa for a few months to see what Quebec will do. I think we can be useful."

He again expressed his fear that Chrétien would win the byelections if the independent MPs resigned. "Think of the message that would send to English Canada. We're pissed off because Meech was defeated, and then we go and elect MPs who screwed us. It doesn't make sense." He told Bourassa he had spoken to Bouchard and that the MP from Lac-Saint-Jean seemed interested. Bourassa responded, yes, it is true, it "might" be useful to defend Quebec's interests. Nothing more. For Lapierre, this was enough to stop him from returning home.

The second MP to receive encouragement from Bourassa that summer was Gilles Rocheleau. Rocheleau was a disciplined and hard-working man, but not the best of speakers. Provocative and biting, he was well known for his frankness and his sense of exaggeration. Born in Hull and an influential businessman in his native city, he was elected a city councillor in 1967, and became mayor in 1974. After seven years as mayor, he moved into provincial politics in 1981, after heading the region's No Committee during the 1980 referendum. From 1985 to 1988 he was supply and services minister in the Bourassa cabinet. After taking part in the birth of Meech on the Quebec side, he was elected a federal MP in 1988 under John Turner's Liberals.

Upon his arrival in Ottawa, Rocheleau was shocked to discover that most of the Liberal caucus was firmly against the Meech Accord. When Turner decided to quit, "it was a mess" behind the closed doors of the caucus. Despite everything, Rocheleau attempted to defend his position. Few MPs were of his opinion, however, and he felt extremely isolated. "It was consummate hypocrisy," he remembers. During the leadership campaign he had no hesitation in supporting Paul Martin who, for one, defended Meech, although this would cost him dearly.

Upon arriving in Calgary for the convention, Rocheleau's decision was clear: he would leave the floor before the winner's hand was raised. He had no intention of being associated with Jean Chrétien, "not even for five minutes!"

If he needed any further convincing, it was provided by Jean Chrétien's heartfelt thanks to Newfoundland Premier Clyde Wells on the convention floor — "Thanks for all you've done, Clyde." After the fact, it was often said that Chrétien was thanking Wells for the support of his Newfoundland delegates, and not for his constitutional position.

For Rocheleau, however, this support was no accident. The two men had the same opinion and their embrace was only a symbol. Chrétien had criticized Meech on the campaign trail, while Martin had faced boos and catcalls across the country because he had stood behind the Accord.

The MP from Hull-Aylmer had already discussed his state of mind with his colleague Lapierre, but had not decided what he would do following the convention. He therefore took a short trip to Vancouver and Victoria before returning to Ottawa. Upon returning, Rocheleau sought out the opinions of many people, including Robert Bourassa. On July 11 he was in Quebec City, where he spent two hours in conversation with his old boss. They discussed a wide range of subjects. "He finally suggested," says Rocheleau, "that, 'in the best interests of Quebec,' I should link up with Bouchard and Lapierre, who were already discussing the question."

Rocheleau was not immediately convinced. After spending years denouncing the "wicked separatists," changing course was no simple thing. Rocheleau was known to be profoundly allergic to the Parti Québécois in any form. He would joke that he used to wake up at nights to hate them. This hatred was legendary; it was his trademark.

During the following weeks he continued to consult his associates, and met first with Jean Lapierre and then with Lucien Bouchard. By August 15, two days after Duceppe's election, the Bloc considered his arrival in their ranks a *fait accompli*. Rocheleau would wait until September 19 before making his move to the sovereignist ranks official, however, in order to keep up "progress in the media."

For Lapierre and Rocheleau, the visit to Bourassa had a clear purpose: to avoid a break with their natural allies. After building their careers by opposing the PQ and the Tories, here they were opting for sovereignty. The choice was a dangerous one since, unlike most Conservatives, they were not returning to nationalist origins. They were taking a greater risk, and they required greater guarantees.

The Three-Step

The meetings with Bourassa reassured the two MPs that they had made the right choice, especially Lapierre who, over the next two years, would act as the real bridge between the small group of Bloc MPs and the Quebec Liberals. To manage this connection, Bourassa assigned Lapierre's old friend Pierre Bibeau, then president of the Olympic Installations Board, and Jean-Claude Rivest, the premier's closest adviser for the previous twenty years.

Until the spring of 1992, Bibeau would serve as backup for Lapierre as he attempted to convince other Liberals to support the Bloc. If people had doubts, Lapierre would gladly tell them to talk to Bibeau. Very few would do so, but those who did found that Bibeau's policy was to say, go ahead.

When the new opposition MPs wanted to ask a question in the Commons, Lapierre was confident he could get the data he needed from Quebec City. Rivest's role was to give Lapierre and the others something to work with. He transmitted information on important questions, organized briefing sessions with ministers like André Bourbeau, in charge of job training, Gérald Tremblay, minister of industry and commerce, or Pierre Paradis, minister of the environment.

Jean-Claude Rivest says that the Quebec government made use of the Bloc MPs in the same way they would have used any opposition members that could be trusted to question the federal government on important matters. "In this case it was the Bloc," he says. "We couldn't trust Chrétien's bunch; they weren't in our gang."

He adds that the major channels of communication remained contacts between Bourassa, Mulroney and their ministers. The Bourassa government also often called upon Conservative senators Solange Chaput-Rolland, Thérèse Lavoie-Roux, Claude Castonguay, Roch Bolduc or Gérald Beaudoin. "From our perspective that was more effective because it was more credible," he adds. Rivest cooperated with Jean Lapierre but not, unless obliged, with the other Bloc members.

Bourassa's goal in aiding Lapierre and the others was to avoid any negative fallout for his party from the Bloc and to put off the new group's inevitable rapprochement with the PQ for as long as possible. He could have dissuaded the two Liberal MPs from joining the Bloc, but he did not even try. His reasoning was simple: the failure of Meech Lake had created frustration in his own caucus and among the public at large, and people needed an outlet for that frustration. The Bloc might serve this role; the important thing was to avoid losing control.

And that was where the two MPs were most useful to Bourassa — as a buffer. Thanks to Lapierre, he knew everything that was going on, much better than if he had to rely on the usual newspaper clippings. Bourassa also knew that Lapierre would not do anything to harm the Quebec Liberal party. "We said to ourselves: he'll let us know if anything rough is likely to happen," says a very close associate of Bourassa. "He was our right-hand man."

Lapierre openly flirted with provincial Liberal MNAs and organized suppers between Bouchard and the Quebec Liberals' youth wing. Bourassa kept a watchful eye. Still, he was not worried. "As long as it's Jean. Jean is part of the family," was the opinion in the Bunker. Bouchard was less welcome, of course, because he was not really trusted. But in any case, Jean was always there. "Our concern was the reaction of the party, the caucus and the government to these meetings. Still we felt that as long as we kept the initiative, there was more to be won by seeing where things were going than lost," the associate continues. They were convinced that in the long term the Bloc would end up in the arms of the PQ, which would discourage Liberals tempted to work with the Bloc. "We thought, our people cannot support the Bloc if its principal ally is our main enemy. The Bloc cannot play both ends against the middle."

The Bloc could also be useful in another way. "It is obvious that these people, as Quebec MPs, were able to ask the government questions; this might not be useful right away, but might be later," reasoned Bourassa at the time. In fact, Bourassa would make few debating points in the Commons as a result, since the Bloc did not have official party standing and so had very limited opportunities to speak. This became clear to the premier very quickly; hence his contacts with the Conservative senators.

Did Bourassa help create the Bloc, thanks to his judicious prodding? "That was not the idea," says Rivest. "We didn't invent the Bloc. There weren't any meetings with Bourassa where people said, hey, we should create a federal sovereignist party. That was never in Bourassa's mind. It was never in my mind. It developed by itself. Once it was there, of course ... We didn't create Lucien Bouchard; that's nonsense. It was the political context; events brought the idea of sovereignty back to the fore."

On the other hand, the effect of Bourassa's attitude cannot be denied. It gave credence to the idea of a rainbow coalition, so dear to Lucien Bouchard and so important for the Bloc's credibility. "To say that Bourassa played a central role would be too strong," says Bouchard for his part. "But he played a role, because [he] gave the green light to those individuals, up to a point [he] gave the cue to people around him."

Launching the Bloc

On July 25, 1990, Bouchard held a press conference to announce the name and mission of his small group as well as Lapierre's arrival. Except for Plamondon, who was on holiday, Bouchard was surrounded by his MPs and his candidate in Laurier–Sainte-Marie. The members of the group who were present — Bouchard, Gérin, Tremblay, Leblanc, Lapierre, Chartrand and Duceppe — explained that they were keeping their House of Commons seats. Making reference to the Bélanger-Campeau Commission, which was to begin hearings in the fall, they first wanted to associate themselves "wholeheartedly with the cooperative process of shaping and building a new Quebec that is in full control of all its powers."

The Bloc was not yet a formal political party. It was still a group of independent MPs who were united by a common purpose. The MPs intended to act as messengers from Quebec to English Canada and establish a new balance of power to ensure that the province's interests and desires were respected.

In the short document released at the press conference in Montreal that day, the Bloc MPs said they intended to:

• act as "spokespeople for Quebec's intentions, in Ottawa and English Canada";

• "ensure that the Quebec people were able to freely exercise their right to self-determination, and strive to have this right understood throughout Canada and respected by federal institutions";

• "promote the emergence of power relationships that would favour Quebec in the implementation of a new political arrangement with its Canadian partner"; and

• "consolidate the Quebec people's political strength and authority at the federal level around Quebec's interests alone."

In addition, they promised that, until sovereignty became a reality, they would demand the share of investment Quebec was entitled to expect from the federal government.

This brief statement was not enough to answer all the questions about the reasons for the Bloc's existence. In the months to come, there would be many times when Lucien Bouchard would have to justify the group's existence and explain what the sovereignists were doing on the federal scene. But this announcement was the start: the formal birth of the Bloc.

3

Crossing the Desert

In September 1990 the Bloc faced its first test. Every day in the House its MPs were compelled to play the same game. In order to be recognized by the Speaker, and so gain the right to speak, they had to play human yo-yo. Stand up. Sit down. Stand up. Sit down. As soon as they arrived in Parliament they realized that, without official party status, they were condemned to the life of the long-distance runner.

The Quebec public was behind them and they could still feel the euphoria of their victory in Laurier–Sainte-Marie, but more often than not they had to content themselves with one meagre question per week, while warming the benches in the farthest corner of the Commons.[1] Procedural wrangling became their daily lot, since it was one of the few ways of attracting attention. They could be heard during the period reserved for MPs' statements or by asking questions or making comments after the speeches of other parliamentarians. But generally the reaction to such remarks was total indifference. As a result, they felt the need for some attention.

Frustrated, their response was often to resort to heckling. Exasperated Bloc MPs would shout across to the opposing benches, make fun of the Tories, and occasionally respond to the insults that came from every side. This lasted from September 1990 to the end of June 1993. The Bloc MPs called it the "crossing of the desert."

Two Years of Frustration

For the first two years, Lapierre was in charge of the game plan. As expected, he got ammunition from his friends in the Quebec Liberals. He still had a tough time putting up with Péquistes, but recognized that it was essential to take into account the other major sovereignist force. It was, after all, the official opposition in the Quebec National Assembly. Since he refused to take part in anything remotely resembling a PQ committee, he limited himself to talking to his Quebec counterpart, PQ house leader Guy Chevrette, on a daily basis.

"It was a daily challenge, to find some way to create a stir, to get press coverage, a sound bite. Every morning was a challenge because there was no way of knowing whether the day would turn out to be nothing but frustration. We had to use every last rule of procedure," Lapierre says. At the same time he was learning those rules; in a few months he learned more than in the preceding thirteen years.

The work was not easy. Lacking a research department, Lapierre and his assistant, Michel Bourque, spent endless hours preparing. Gilles Duceppe and his staff would often help out. At first the Bloc MPs were optimistic, since soon after arriving in September they succeeded in forcing the House to take a position on an amendment to Bill C-44, which approved the Hibernia megaproject, involving the construction and exploitation of a drilling platform off New-foundland. The bill was tabled as soon as the House reopened. Plamondon thought it unacceptable that the first reward should be handed to Clyde Wells, an opponent of the Meech Lake Accord, and, worse still, that nothing in the project guaranteed any spinoffs for Canada. He proposed that the bill include "in particular the assurance that tenders for the platform's five supermodules be reserved, to start with, for Canadian companies only." The other three parties found themselves in a corner, which in itself was enough to please the Bloc.

The Bloc again managed to attract attention in 1992 with a barrage of statements attacking the federal referendum act. It was one of their rare successes. The Bloc MPs spent more time asking to be recognized by the Speaker than they did actually taking part in House debates. And, when they did address the House, more often than not it was a total loss.

From June 1991 to June 1993, the Bloc asked 86 questions: 58 while Jean Lapierre was house leader and 28 under the leadership of Louis Plamondon. Not much in two years. Bloc MPs, eager to be noticed, took advantage of the period reserved for MPs' statements on 63 occasions. Duceppe, with 20 statements, and Leblanc, with 25, made the most use of this method.[2]

The process remained frustrating, however, since it led to few results. Bouchard has very bad memories of those three years in the House. "It was terrible; it was rough," he says. "We would be insulted; no one would answer our questions; we would be given half a question at 2:45 in the afternoon. Everyone would have left; all the reporters were gone. In the general confusion we would be allowed one question, *the* question of the week. Then the minister would rise, and treat us like kids." Determined not to be ignored, Lapierre's staff got into the habit of warning reporters in advance whenever a Bloc MP was going to ask a question, thus encouraging them to stay until the end of Question Period.

Rocheleau, who lived only a stone's throw from Parliament Hill, was in the House almost every day and got the chance to experience everyone's frustration. "It was incredibly unpleasant, and stressful, too. You had to listen to all sorts of crazy things, but you couldn't respond."

The NDP was the worst tormentor. Bouchard, like his MPs, thinks they were "the worst double-crossers ... You couldn't count on them. They would pretend to help us, but when push came to shove, they would do the opposite. Oh, the NDP — everybody has bad memories of the NDP. The NDP are disagreeable customers in the House," Bouchard remembers, darkly.

Every Bloc MP recalls the occasion in November 1990 when the Bloc made an arrangement with the New Democrats before presenting an anti-strikebreaker bill. The NDP had promised to support the Bloc, but when the time came they simply disappeared. The New Democrats, tired of hearing the Bloc MPs shouting from behind them, lost patience and started insulting them in return. "They were really vicious to the Bloc," says Rocheleau, remembering all the insults: "Bunch of separatists!", "Parasites!"

Duceppe almost came to blows with New Democrat Jim Fulton in the opposition anteroom. MP for Skeena in B.C., Fulton had said that he agreed with people who said that Quebec had blood on its hands because of the Great Whale project. Fulton explained to journalists that he was referring to the blood of fish and birds, but Duceppe, like others, thought that Fulton was speaking of native blood. He could not tolerate the innuendo in the B.C. MP's remark.

The Tories and the Liberals did not show any greater sympathy. Like the NDP, they refused to allow the Bloc members to be consulted on the workings of the House. They regularly opposed giving the Bloc the right to speak. A few MPs were more open, including Liberal Marcel Prud'homme, who came to their defence on several occasions. Conservative Guy Saint-Julien went so far as to give up his right to speak in some committees to allow the Bloc MPs to take a position on some bills of particular interest to Quebec.

"This was not a particularly easy period. We did not have much opportunity to express ourselves in the Commons, or in committees of the House," Leblanc explains. "We almost stopped attending committees altogether. Essentially they were not giving us the right to speak. We were always the last to be given a chance; if there was some time left at the end, then we could speak. After a while we said to ourselves, well, OK, if that's the way it is."

This lack of enthusiasm was a growing problem by early 1991. The Bloc MPs simply reacted to events: the budget, the Spicer Commission, federal constitutional proposals, the Beaudoin-Dobbie Report, constitutional negotiations, and so on. Without resources or opportunities to speak, they had no control over events. These were the most difficult eighteen months. Bloc MPs were increasingly absent from the Commons, as each one searched for a role. The former Tories let their parliamentary duties drop in favour of work in their ridings, and efforts to change their movement into a party.

This situation was not without consequences. In a stinging article in *Le Journal de Montréal*, journalist Michel C. Auger criticized the chronic absenteeism of some Bloc members. He was not the only person to notice. The subject was such a tricky one that the Bloc began to fear it would become an election issue in 1993. In a note sent to Bouchard just before the leaders' debate, his own staff estimated that he had missed 82 per cent of roll-call votes between May 13, 1991, and June 1, 1992. The Bloc was able to find a response: Mulroney had missed 84 per cent!

The situation created tensions among MPs. Lapierre felt very isolated, but "kept his eye on the puck." Rocheleau occasionally lost patience, and took the liberty of calling the less dedicated to order. Bouchard, who had been busy with the Bélanger-Campeau Commission from November 1990 to March 1991, disappeared July 1 to write his autobiography. For ten months this was his main activity, and he remembers the period with enthusiasm. Benoît Tremblay found Bélanger-Campeau fascinating, and spent most of his time on it in the fall of 1990. After that he followed the example of most of his former Tory colleagues and worked mainly towards turning the Bloc into a party. Plamondon, a born organizer, put most of his efforts there as well. Leblanc, an unassuming personality, did the same, but was nonetheless more often in the House.

"We went through the winter, and it was tough," Plamondon remembers. "Lapierre took all the questions, made all the statements. We were totally isolated. But we worked on organizing, always organizing, along with a small fundraising drive, and we tried to get by." As for Gérin, he was absent more and more often. Over his last year he appeared in the Commons no more than half a dozen times.

In Quebec City the limits of the Bloc's situation soon became evident. Support for Lapierre was still forthcoming, but increasing reliance was put on the personal relationship between Bourassa and Mulroney, and on the Conservative senators.

Lapierre had come to count on Duceppe's help, but this became less and less possible. At the beginning of 1991, Bouchard had chosen Duceppe to represent the Bloc within Mouvement Québec, an organization established in the wake of Bélanger-Campeau to pressure Bourassa to hold a referendum on sovereignty. Duceppe left to tour various Quebec regions, and this kept him away from the House.

The other MPs made occasional appearances. Between trips and speeches, Bouchard would show up when he thought it politic — to answer the Tories following the presentation of their constitutional proposals or after the Beaudoin-Dobbie Report. "I took part in our denunciations of these reports, but really that was about it," he admits.

At Each Other's Throats

This difficult situation had two results. To begin with, Bouchard believes that the hostility of the other parties "put gas in our tank ... When they gave us a rough time in the Commons, we would say to ourselves, we'll be back, we'll back with our own people, and they won't be there any more ... Honestly, I am sure we wouldn't have been so motivated if they had been nice to us ... But they hated us so much, they couldn't do anything else."

The second effect was a negative one. The difficulties in the House heightened personality conflicts among the disparate individuals in the Bloc, people who had been brought together by circumstances alone. Tensions began to grow as early as the summer of 1990, although the Bloc was flying high at the time. The caucus was literally divided into two groups: Bouchard and Lapierre on one side, later to be joined by Duceppe and Rocheleau, and all of Bouchard's former Tory colleagues on the other. The only person who got along with everyone was Louis Plamondon.

The way that Lapierre joined the Bloc caused the first reaction. As he said himself, he only took Lucien Bouchard into account when the time came to choose a name for the group and define its mission. Lapierre went straight to the leader, and did not ask what the others thought. The leader was the leader. As for Bouchard, he did not even bother to consult the others when drawing up the mission statement with Lapierre.

The former Conservatives found out about the document in Benoît Tremblay's living room, just a few hours before the press conference on July 25. Only one person was absent: Plamondon had taken ten days off. Gérin, Tremblay, Chartrand and Leblanc were faced with a *fait accompli*. The press releases were already prepared. They found out that Lapierre would be Bloc house leader by reading the press release.

They were stunned. A mission statement and a division of tasks were being imposed on them without consultation. Gérin was furious. Leblanc and Tremblay did not at all appreciate being taken for granted. And yet all three were pleased to have Lapierre join them and would have gladly accepted him as house leader. It was just too much to have him forced on them in this way.

Lapierre says that he was surprised at the reaction and did not understand what was going on. For him, if the leader was in agreement, the rest of the troops should follow. "Personally, if I joined, it was because I had a deal with him," says Lapierre. "The others, well, logically, he spoke for them." He negotiated two items with Bouchard: the statement, and the position as house leader. He wanted the group to act as if it had a formal existence. The less-than-warm reception took him by surprise. He had thought that everything was resolved, and yet here he was in the middle of a dispute. Asking himself exactly what he was doing there, he considered walking out.

In the end the MPs negotiated acceptable titles for themselves. Gérin would be in charge of relations with sovereignist groups, Leblanc would be caucus chair, Tremblay would cover economic questions, and Plamondon would be responsible for organization. Since they were in the middle of an election campaign — not the time to appear divided — the group worked out a compromise, changed the press releases and held the press conference. Duceppe and Rocheleau, who joined the group in August, were not involved in this altercation, but they could feel its effects.

As for Gilbert Chartrand, he was almost always absent and on the sidelines. In any case, he would return to the Conservative fold in April 1991, even before the Bloc was established as an official party. Chartrand never explained the fundamental reasons for his action, but some people, including Plamondon, mention financial difficulties.

The other Conservatives stayed in the Bloc's ranks, but would never have very cordial relations with Lapierre, who, for his part, thinks this was inevitable. "In any case, things could never have been different," he says, "because the situation was unnatural. We were not politically active for the same reasons, or in the same ways."

Plamondon, too, thinks that divisions were to be expected among MPs who had come from different parties and who had different opinions on the major questions of the day, such as the GST, free trade, funding of political parties, and so on. "The worst of it was, you had Tories who hated Liberals, and had always hated them, and Liberals who had lost their jobs to Tories and who had always hated the PQ. Well, put all that together ... And these were strong personalities, too."

The tensions and personality conflicts were sharp enough to reach the ears of Bourassa and of the PQ's strategy committee, which met every Monday morning. "Everyone knew that Bouchard was stuck with a troublesome caucus," recalls a close adviser of Parizeau. "There were complaints about how difficult it was to manage."

Plamondon was the only one to escape the divisive atmosphere. Cheerful by nature, he was always ready with a joke. Not only was he a good organizer, dedicated and hardworking, but he was also an expert at patching up difficult relationships. When a fire broke out, more often than not he would be the one called to put it out. And since peacemaking was in his character, he would gladly accept the challenge.

Gérin, Tremblay and Leblanc, for their parts, all had personalities that had difficulty working with those of Bouchard and Lapierre. As for Rocheleau and Duceppe, they were lucky enough to arrive after the first disputes. Rocheleau was a disciplined and pragmatic MP who liked to see people do the work they had been assigned. A longtime Liberal, he naturally had closer affinities with Lapierre. He did his work, occasionally admonished his colleagues, and did not try to occupy a larger place than was necessary. People were not led to envy him. In the Bloc he was recognized as a straight shooter.

Duceppe was a newly elected MP, and determined to take his proper place in the House. As a result he was very active in Ottawa. A former union negotiator, he was methodical and used to working long hours, qualities that he would be helpful in the Commons. Lapierre was more than happy to have a helper and became a friend. The trade unionist and the former assistant to André Ouellet share certain ideas and have similar ways of working. Lapierre considers that, above all, they have the same sense of mission. Duceppe quickly became the Bloc's second spokesperson, after Lapierre. Plamondon was sympathetic, but the others, Gérin in particular, were not so pleased.

Still more important, Duceppe showed unwavering loyalty to Bouchard, which rapidly earned him the leader's confidence. Bouchard likes soldiers who are loyal and who do not try to take command. This is Duceppe's character and is one reason why he found himself at the Mouvement Québec rather than Gérin, although the latter was officially in charge of links with sovereignist groups.

As for Gérin, he was a real problem as far as Bouchard was concerned. Despite his services over the years, the Bloc leader could no longer tolerate him. Lapierre felt the same. The three men were at such loggerheads that Gérin would stop attending the House of Commons altogether.

Gérin was the archetypal loner. He would make decisions without consulting anyone, even those affected, and had connections with Bernard Landry, which irritated Bouchard. "He is not a team player," says one of Bouchard's first collaborators. "And he is not easy to understand, either."

Often, when defending a point, Gérin would claim to have Landry's support, which amuses the PQ minister. "I was present in the Bloc despite myself," he says, "because they were having internal struggles. One side would claim I was behind them, when in fact I had no presence and didn't want one. Let's say I was a useful personality. It was easy to say: Landry told me — Landry said we should —" Landry says he reached agreement with Bouchard to let the Bloc leader deal with his own affairs. From then on, any relations between them would be of an official nature, between PQ vice-president and Bloc leader.

Gérin states, however, that he maintained contact with the PQ vice-president until 1993. Bouchard suspected this, and these suspicions were confirmed when he learned that Gérin had attended the Parti Québécois eleventh national convention in late January 1991.

Gérin's actions created waves in the group, since Bouchard, anxious to maintain the Bloc's nonpartisan image, had told his MPs not to attend PQ meetings unless they were already PQ members, which was the case for Duceppe and Tremblay.

Still at the PQ convention, Gérin let slip to journalists that the fate of the Bloc depended on Lucien Bouchard's decision whether or not to continue after June 1991. As for Gérin, he would be very disappointed if the group did not transform itself into a party. This question was still the subject of hot debates inside the Bloc, and Bouchard had not yet taken a public position on the issue.[3]

It would be three days later, during a break in proceedings at the Bélanger-Campeau Commission, before Bouchard would talk for the first time of creating a party and running candidates in the next federal election.[4] Although his mind had been made up, Bouchard did not appreciate his MP campaigning in the press and giving the impression that Bouchard was responding to pressure. But Gérin did not stop there. Next he declared it was no secret that Bouchard was more interested in a political career in Quebec than in Ottawa. The remark came at an unfortunate moment, while tensions were brewing between Bouchard and Parizeau at the Bélanger-Campeau Commission.

In early April when the PQ confirmed that it intended to help the Bloc in future federal elections, Gérin once again caused problems. He went so far as to accept his PQ membership card directly from Landry and Parizeau, and in front of the television cameras to boot. "As if Bernard Landry just happens to carry membership cards in his pocket," fumes a close associate of Bouchard, even today.

Gérin's act posed a problem for several MPs. Plamondon was asked why he didn't do the same thing. He was forced to explain, yet again, that the Bloc's intention was to bring together all sovereignists, no matter what their allegiance in Quebec provincial politics. Gérin also took advantage of the PQ national council to state that "the Bloc will do everything it can to help the PQ in the provincial election."[5] Not only did his statement put Bouchard in a difficult position, it also affected Lapierre and Rocheleau, who were still members of the Quebec Liberal party.

In the next few days, Bouchard was obliged to clarify things. He expressed his gratitude for the PQ's support, but also said there was no question of returning the favour during the provincial election, since he was also looking for support from the Quebec Liberals. "Gérin had never mentioned the question to Lucien," remembers Lapierre, "so it is not surprising that he was shocked."

"There were some serious confrontations at the time," Gérin admits. Not only did Gérin maintain his connections with the PQ, but he was getting on his boss's nerves with his constant pressure to form a party. "Towards the end, my relations with Lucien Bouchard gave me the impression he could not accept the fact that I had done everything in my power to reach my goals. He felt pressured." But

Gérin refused to let the leader's hesitation stop him. "I said to myself, we aren't going to do nothing just because Lucien Bouchard can't make up his mind, or because Lucien Bouchard doesn't want [a party]."

Bouchard could tolerate Gérin less and less. He considered expelling him on several occasions. "Bouchard was so sick of him that he would have been content if Gérin had simply resigned," says Stéphane Le Bouyonnec. Vice-president and managing director of the Groupe Conseil Innovitech, Le Bouyonnec participated closely in the organizing of the Bloc from summer 1991 to June 1992. The Bloc leader also got wind of Gérin's ambitions to run at the provincial level under the PQ banner, a plan that did not, in fact, come to fruition. The hostility between Gérin and Bouchard became so serious that they stopped talking to each other completely. Plamondon, often called on to intervene, remembers that their final conversations were stormy.

He remembers what he believes was the last exchange between the two men. Bouchard, he says, "argued with Gérin and called me afterwards to say, 'I had a big argument with Gérin. I just about told him to piss off. Would you see what you can do?'" Plamondon tried, but Gérin was furious. He said he was not about to forget.

Gérin was also angry with Bouchard for not recognizing everything that he had done for the leader in the past and for favouring Duceppe. "He wanted to be in charge of the Bloc's public relations with the other movements, especially the Parti Québécois," says Plamondon. "He wanted to be the Bloc's number two spokesman, but all that was given to Duceppe."

Gérin did not run for the Bloc in 1993, returning instead to his law practice. It was some time before Bouchard would speak to him again. At a Sherbrooke, Quebec party function after the October 1993 election, Bouchard publicly thanked Gérin for his efforts, giving him some credit for the birth of the Bloc. Gérin was in the hall, and at the end of the meeting approached Bouchard to shake hands. But that was the extent of it.

Things did not work out between Gérin and Lapierre either. Gérin did not like the way Lapierre always pushed himself to the forefront, grabbing all the media attention. Lapierre, for his part, was allergic to Gérin's machinations with the PQ. He was determined to maintain his Liberal links. Of course, Lapierre's position was contradictory, since he himself was doing everything he could to encourage meetings between Bouchard and Quebec Liberal MNAs. For the same reasons, in the spring of 1991 he met with Mario Dumont, the new president of the Liberal youth wing. His goal, he told Dumont, was to broaden the Bloc's membership to include people with "a less obtuse vision of sovereignty than the PQ."

The two men met on a number of occasions, even becoming friends. Eventually Lapierre advised a sceptical Dumont to meet with Bouchard directly. For this purpose he organized a supper at Milos Restaurant on Park Avenue in Montreal. He invited Michel Bissonnette, Dumont's predecessor at the Liberal youth wing, to join them. Lapierre would repeat this experience with some dozen Quebec Liberal members.

As far as Lapierre was concerned, it was essential to maintain these links, since the very idea of ending up in the PQ's hands was completely distasteful to him. Gérin, for his part, felt that the Parti Québécois was central to the Bloc's future. As a result, each was suspicious of the other's manoeuvring.

"He wanted to deliver the whole gang to the PQ," says Lapierre. "I didn't care if he ended up there himself, although it often bothered Lucien more than me. As far as I was concerned, Gérin could do whatever he wanted with the PQ."

Gérin, on the other hand, thought that Lapierre had a mandate from Bourassa to "neutralize the relationship between the Bloc and the PQ." Hence his decision to accept the PQ membership card. "I said to Monsieur Parizeau that I would do it at the most opportune moment," says Gérin. "And [I] agreed with Bernard Landry to send a clear signal that showed a Bloc member was also in the PQ. That caused problems because it helped to clarify something that was unclear. No one could criticize my action, and that sent out a clear public signal, one that was consistent with my strategy."

Relations between Lucien Bouchard and Benoît Tremblay were never as hostile, but they were never warm either. Tremblay was a former professor at the École des Hautes Études Commerciales in Montreal. Bouchard recognized his intelligence and extensive knowledge of economic matters, but sometimes found him unwilling to work particularly hard and considered him inconsistent. The leader's entourage were harsher in their judgement. Some were easily prepared to describe him as lazy, disconcerting and easily influenced. Tremblay was also thought to be "under François Gérin's thumb." The two men would occasionally have a few drinks together, and the leader was concerned that their discretion could suffer.

For a time, however, Tremblay seemed to be in Bouchard's good graces. It was Tremblay who proposed Duceppe as a candidate, and who went with Bouchard to Bob Dufour's brasserie. Tremblay was also the one to follow the proceedings of the Bélanger-Campeau Commission, going through its documents, providing summaries to the others, keeping them up to date, and doing the groundwork for the Bloc's own statement to the Commission. His office was without a single free chair or table; documents were everywhere.

In December, however, when Bouchard was absent from the Commission because of a European trip, it was Duceppe who was chosen to replace him as commissioner. Bouchard considered him to be more disciplined. He had complete confidence in Duceppe, but not in Tremblay. Plamondon could see that Tremblay was very offended, and asked Bouchard the reason for his decision. He answered that Duceppe was the only MP actually elected under the Bloc banner, which gave him greater legitimacy. "The reasoning was sound enough, but," Plamondon believes, "it was also because Bouchard was close to Duceppe."

Gérin is more cynical. Since Bouchard dislikes strong characters, he could not choose Tremblay. "It could have led to problems," he says. "But Duceppe, he's always operated in step with Lucien." Tremblay never had good relations with Duceppe; in fact, the reverse was true. In Bouchard's entourage this was seen as proof that he was "spiteful" and "jealous."

Whatever the case, Tremblay was thought to be unpredictable. The proof cited is his absence when it was time to respond to the 1991 budget speech. On that occasion the Speaker of the House decided to give the Bloc a turn to speak. Tremblay, the Bloc's economic critic, was absent, however, and the Bloc was forced to pass once or twice. Duceppe considered it ridiculous that the Bloc, after all its complaints of not being heard, should refuse to speak when given the chance. Furious, he decided to respond to the minister of finance himself. Tremblay was displeased, since the economy was his department. Tremblay would only rarely regain any interest in the work of the House, even after the 1993 federal election.

Nic Leblanc never had any conflicts with Bouchard, but he never really had his respect, either. Leblanc was the former director of the Quebec Chamber of Commerce, and also former president of the South Shore Chamber. A reserved person, he spoke rarely and was conservative in his views. He was not the type to juggle theories and ideas, nor was he a notable speaker. He did not impress the Bloc leader and was out of his depth when faced with this jumble of antagonisms. He liked things to be organized and predictable, which explains why he was so eager for a meeting of the former Conservatives after their resignations.

Bouchard knew of Leblanc's right-wing ideas and did not share them. This was one reason why he did not consult his caucus before drawing up the Bloc's mission statement. He preferred to impose his position rather than negotiate every comma with people whom he doubted, in some cases, were able to understand the subtleties involved.

Bouchard never criticized his MPs in public; instead, he simply admitted that there was disagreement. "It was already obvious that we were not all on the same wavelength," he says. This explains in part why for a long time he refused to come up with a common platform. "I could see that Nic and I clearly had different ideas, and I did not see how it was possible to agree on a common party platform."

Some people, however, remember virulent attacks made in private against some MPs. Bouchard's imagination had no limits when the time came to find fault, one witness remembers, and there was no shortage of insults and curses. For Bouchard, some were lazy, others could not be trusted, while others had harebrained ideas or lacked discipline and weren't conscientious. Gérin was subject to the worst insults: "Double-dealer, devil, troublemaker" in the caucus. Plamondon was the only former Tory to be seen with some favour. As for Lapierre, he could get into heaven without talking to St. Peter.

An intelligent tactician, Lapierre was a pleasant and likeable companion who knew how to win over his audience. He had a lot of influence. His ideas, even the most off-the-wall, were assured of Bouchard's attention, while any project that Lapierre already opposed would be likely to be opposed by Bouchard as well. "During that whole first year," Plamondon remarks, "Duceppe and Lapierre were Bouchard's only two close advisers in the Bloc." As a result, the other MPs felt left out. "He distrusted his caucus," says Le Bouyonnec.

Friction between the various MPs became so intense that Jean Fournier, party organizer in 1991 and 1992, felt obliged to speak to Bouchard. Fournier tried to persuade the leader that he should not ignore his caucus, but to no avail.

"At various times we presented plans to Bouchard that would have allowed the MPs to play a role in the various commissions," states

Le Bouyonnec. "The idea was to better integrate the caucus and the party apparatus. He wasn't interested, so we were obliged to act on the sly."

In private, Lapierre expressed the same lack of respect for his colleagues, but he did so less sharply than his boss. Even today he will explain that he hesitated to join the group in the first place because he had nothing to gain from associating with a "mutual admiration society." For Lapierre they were "a frustrated little gang" with whom he had nothing in common and whom he considered "politically ignorant." "I didn't need to go to Marriage Encounter!"

He is unable to talk about their meeting in Nic Leblanc's office in Longueuil without scorn. "They made [Bouchard] leader, but leader of — nothing." For Lapierre, they chose Bouchard as their "big chief," their "pseudoleader." What's more, he says he was not very impressed with their resignations. "They weren't effective actions. There were no decent sound bites to be had." He had doubts about his future colleagues' intentions. He says that they had no reason to unite. They simply wanted to get back at the Conservatives, to create "a negative organization at Mulroney's expense." He wasn't interested.

Yet in 1990, when the former Tories resigned, they had all praised Mulroney's efforts and promised to support him when he proposed policies that favoured Quebec. Some still praised the prime minister. In fact, it was Lapierre, who says he did not want to create a group founded on anti-Mulroneyism, who had a hard time associating with these former Mulroney supporters. "I was in the opposition, and I hated the Conservatives in any shape or form," he says. He felt closer to the provincial Liberals.

When he approached Bouchard, before resigning from the federal Liberals, he made his position clear: "I think we have nothing in common, but perhaps, over the next period, while we wait to see what they do to Quebec, we can certainly give them a really hard time."

Lapierre was no more conciliatory when he explained to the former Tories why he wanted the post of house leader. "You guys have a problem," he said, "you get weak in the knees when you look at your old friends. You say hello, you chat. I'm sorry, I already hate them. I won't be afraid to give it to them!"

The polls were what saved the Bloc in the face of all this internecine sniping. Every month it was the same story: the Bloc and their leader were winning the battle for public opinion.[6] As well, there were some successes, including Pierrette Venne's arrival in August 1991, thanks to another of Gérin's manoeuvres.

Venne was MP for Saint-Hubert, and she had stood out among Conservatives by taking a strong stand in favour of tough firearms restrictions. A nationalist, she walked out at the Tories' Toronto convention after the delegates rejected her plan to divide the country into five regions. The only woman in the Bloc's caucus, she had more affinity with the former Tories, who had been her caucus colleagues. On good terms with everyone, she would avoid the quarrels that divided her new allies.

* * *

The frustration in the House, the antipathy and the envy that developed between the MPs, Bouchard's lack of interest in settling disputes, and his own involvement in some of them would all work against the Bloc during the first two years of its existence, slowing down organization and financing. Tormented by ambivalence, Bouchard had difficulty adjusting to being a leader, to being responsible for a party, to having a caucus to administer. It was against this backdrop of tensions and indecision that the debate around the creation of a real party began.

4

The End of the Rainbow

It was hardly surprising that the group of eight MPs had so much difficulty in agreeing to transform the Bloc into a political party since the ideological divisions among them were marked. The subject became yet another source of disagreement. On the one hand were the former Tories. They wanted to create a properly organized party, one that Gérin and Leblanc hoped would be close to the Parti Québécois. On the other side were Rocheleau, who was sceptical and not interested in creating a PQ subsidiary, and Bouchard, Lapierre and Duceppe, who opposed the idea vehemently. They preferred to build a nonpartisan movement — a rainbow coalition — with relatively loose structures.

The Bloc had begun on the basis that it was an informal group of MPs without a party line but with one common objective: to defend Quebec's interests. Tremblay thinks it was logical that the group began in this way. Bouchard, he says, "was not prepared to commit himself for three years, given the highly unstable nature of the situation. Essentially the decision to act over a longer period was taken step by step, in order to keep everyone content."

Following the Longueuil meeting on June 29, 1990, events continued to unfold, and no one was bothered about structures. The campaign in Laurier–Sainte-Marie, the official arrival of Lapierre, Duceppe's election, Rocheleau's arrival, the favourable opinion polls, and the start of work at the Bélanger-Campeau Commission were more than enough to keep everyone busy.

"But at a certain moment you have to get organized," says Tremblay. In the fall of 1990, the discussion began. Once again Gérin was the first to move, insisting on a fundraising drive. Duceppe was not interested, since he was in the process of raising money to cover the cost of his own office. Lapierre did not want to hear about it either. "We each pay our own way," he said. The others were talking about fundraising, "collecting a million dollars." He couldn't believe his ears. "What's going on?" he asked. "I just got out of one political party, and I'm not going to get caught up again. We all pay our own way. We are independents who simply unite for common purposes."

Plamondon agreed that the Bloc needed a financial basis, especially to pay the leader's expenses. Bouchard was constantly being called upon to speak, and Plamondon considered it unacceptable to see his leader going to speaking engagements by bus.

"Lucien does not have much money," explained the MP for Richelieu. "His salary has dropped to $60,000, his wife does not work outside the home, and he has two children. He doesn't have his limousine any more, and he has to make do with less than half the salary [he had as a minister]. And he has to speak everywhere. He must pay for his hotel, transportation, expenses. That is why we need funds."

Bouchard hesitated. He disliked fundraising intensely, and he had better things to do at the Bélanger-Campeau Commission. The discussions broke down over the type of fundraising to be used. Gérin was determined to hold out for grass roots donations from individuals only. The Liberals found this position purist. The group decided to put off the decision. In any case, no one was fooled: A fundraising drive leads inevitably to the creation of a party.

Persuading the Leader

Leblanc was among those who believed strongly in the idea of a party, with members, riding associations, fundraising, and nominating conventions to choose candidates for the next elections. He maintained that, without all this, the group would soon be ignored: no one would take them seriously. They needed a structure that people could identify with, was his belief.

Tremblay agreed:

> The aim was to broaden the base of people working for
> Quebec sovereignty. We knew that the Bloc had won the
> support of many people who were not yet ready — a
> certain number are still not ready — to join the Parti
> Québécois. The Bloc gave them a forum. The goal was to
> provide a democratic forum that could mobilize such peo-
> ple and allow them to progress in this option. I think that
> was the essential idea behind forming a political party, to
> give people who were not yet prepared to join the PQ a
> right to speak, to give them a forum and to mobilize them
> for concrete action.

Rocheleau, always pragmatic, simply wanted to be certain that they knew what they were doing. He had no interest in working to build a structure that would then collapse. "Because it's one hell of a job," he says. "It took a lot of work." Looking back, he is surprised that such a small and divided group was able to manage it. "We still weren't quite operating as a coherent group." He wanted certain guarantees. He wanted to know if the grass roots were really interested. He suggested that they begin doing groundwork in the ridings to see if the desire for a party existed. Rocheleau also wanted nothing to do with "some kind of Ottawa branch of the Parti Québécois." That was not why he joined the Bloc.

The greatest resistance came from Bouchard and Lapierre. Although Bouchard had said as early as the fall of 1990 that the Bloc was not just a flash in the pan, a "passing fancy," he was not prepared to make the jump to a formal party.[1] He showed his ambivalence in an interview with journalist Michel Vastel on January 15, 1991: "I told the Bloc MPs I was prepared to stay for a year, and that when summer came we'd reevaluate. In the meantime, the Bloc has to act. There are people ready to work, to organize and to raise funds. I still haven't given the green light. The others have to decide. In late spring or summer we will be in a better position to judge both the Bloc's situation and mine. Then we'll see what happens."

Bouchard kept the brakes on until the last minute, as he puts it, waging "a final struggle to prevent the Bloc from turning into a party ... More or less unconsciously, I knew very well that if I started a party, I would be compelled to remain in politics. I could not set up a party, get people to join it, convince candidates to run, and then, after all that, keep open the possibility that I might not run again in the next elections. I had to make my own political commitment. Since I had not really decided to stay in politics for the long haul, for a significant length of time," he adds, "I resisted the idea of forming a party."

Jean Lapierre strengthened any doubts Bouchard had. He reminded Bouchard vigorously that, if Bouchard moved towards founding a party, as its founder he would have no choice but to stay on. Bouchard had another fear. He wondered what the PQ's reaction would be. "I did not want to get into the PQ's bad books. At the time the PQ wanted the Bloc to exist, but a lot of people in the PQ distrusted the idea. Not everyone was convinced."

Francine Lalonde, the Bloc MP for Mercier, was then a member of the PQ executive. She remembers that people had mixed feelings.

Some were pleased to finally have a sovereignist wing in Ottawa, but others were worried, because the Bloc "had not been set up by the usual supporters of sovereignty. People were concerned about the strength of the Bloc's support for sovereignty, about the depth of their commitment."

Bouchard could feel this suspicion. "At the beginning not everyone was as convinced as Monsieur Parizeau. He was clear from the start. Others were reticent or worried. They said to themselves: We've often sent Quebecers to Ottawa, really good people, and the system has always swallowed them up, sending them back as adversaries," Bouchard explains, referring to the Conservatives of the *beau risque*.

"We had legitimate doubts about the solidity of Bouchard's conversion and his constancy, which was understandable because he had changed his mind several times, had been in different camps and groups, and the *beau risque*, and this and that," recounts Bernard Landry.

During the Bélanger-Campeau Commission, several of the orthodox sovereignists were worried. "We don't want to be dragged into another *beau risque*. We were taken once. We won't let ourselves be taken a second time," explained Landry. And the fact that Bouchard supported at the time a different strategy from that of Parizeau did not reassure the sceptics.

For strategic reasons, Parizeau hoped for the creation of a party on the federal scene, but he left it in Bouchard's hands. "Monsieur Parizeau really did not get involved," says Bouchard. "Honestly, he was really very correct throughout the whole process. He took no part in all the discussion. Essentially he gave me a free hand and told me that whatever I decided to do would be all right."

Among Parizeau's entourage, people were not worried by the Bloc leader's hesitations. By late summer 1990 they were convinced that Bouchard understood the need for a party. They understood that any doubts he had were personal in nature. "I'm doing this out of a sense of duty, because you know that for me, the law ..." Bouchard confided to Parizeau even before the Bélanger-Campeau Commission.

Tremblay, Leblanc, Plamondon and Gérin knew that Bouchard was hesitant. As Bélanger-Campeau drew to a close, they decided to put on the pressure. Gérin began the dance by making public statements as early as January 1991 that forced Bouchard to get involved. Next it was the other MPs' turn. They informed Bouchard that they intended to create a party and asked him if he wished to be its leader.

For Benoît Tremblay, action was essential. "People were prepared to go on precisely because we organized ourselves as a party, [said] we would run candidates everywhere, etc., etc. You can't mobilize people to go nowhere. Of course, if you mobilize people you need a vehicle to travel in. This is precisely why I stayed, and why as early as '91 we had to set up some structure, so that the movement could have a political presence on the federal scene."

The former Tory MPs worked hard to create the momentum that would overcome the resistance of Bouchard, Lapierre and Duceppe. They mobilized the people around them and interest increased rapidly. People began contacting them, offering to be candidates in the next federal election. The first one was Denis Vallée, a businessman from Sainte-Marie-de-Beauce who was close to the PQ. He wrote to the Bloc in January 17, 1991. When, at the end of January 1991, Bouchard publicly discussed the possibility of having candidates, the offers multiplied. Former PQ MNA Maurice Dupré wrote to Bouchard on April 8, 1991 to let him know he was available. Antoine Dubé, the Bloc MP for Lévis, put his name on the list of potential candidates as early as May 17, 1991.

Lapierre disagreed entirely with the party project. He did not want the discipline of a party. He would have preferred that the group restrict itself to its policy of defending Quebec's interests. He considered this to be the only way to respect everyone's ideological differences.

"Let's not try to be identical, to make people believe we agree on everything," he said. "We have only one thing in common: to defend Quebec, to be there to defend Quebec's interests." He finally gave in, after strong resistance, only because the pressure was too great, and because he realized that some MPs "needed it." So he said, "If they want it, I'll go along, but they shouldn't count on my help."

Plamondon promised that Lapierre would not have to do a thing, that he would organize the founding convention and take care of financing it. He kept his word. To reassure suppliers, however, Plamondon had to put his personal signature on $18,000 worth of bills. Luckily, he was not required to pay a single one, since the event was a success and brought in more than it cost.

In the spring of 1991, the question was finally decided. There would be a party. The next debate then began: what type of structure should they set up? What should the membership policy be? As always, some people wanted a very flexible organization, while others pushed for something more elaborate. To avoid putting the whole project off indefinitely, the eight MPs finally agreed on a half-and-half solution that would include commissions where nominations would be standard procedure and votes would be rare. Since some people were still dragging their feet, they played with the terminology, talking about sympathizers rather than members.

At least, something was happening. Bouchard asked Yvan Loubier, on the research team for the nonaligned group at the Bélanger-Campeau Commission, and Georges Mathews, of the Institut National de Recherche Scientifique in Montreal, to draw up a new manifesto. According to the authors, the loyalty of the best-intentioned Québécois could not help but become "diluted," "superficial," "crushed," and "co-opted" within federalist parties. The Bloc was presented as a way of reestablishing "harmony, legitimacy and balance between what the Quebec people want and the actions of its representatives on the federal scene," and of "making the voice of the real Quebec heard."

The manifesto stated that the Bloc's role was to make Canada understand Quebec's determination to achieve sovereignty. It was to explain the economic, political and social realities of the province and facilitate future negotiations between Canada and a sovereign Quebec. The document went so far as to say that it wanted to show Canadians that sovereignty was an opportunity for them, because they could then fashion their country in their own image.

The Bloc also published a milder document for the public, entitled *Vers le nécessaire rassemblement des souverainistes à Ottawa* (The need for sovereignists to become a force in Ottawa). In it, Bloc Québécois members maintained that Quebec MPs who served in the major federal parties always ended up being co-opted and defending Ottawa's interests rather Quebec's. As proof, they offered the fact that most Conservatives did not react to the failure of Meech in the same was as the majority of Québécois.

"With the advent of the Bloc Québécois, it will no longer be possible to use federal MPs from Quebec to 'keep Quebec in its place.' Quebec will never again tolerate a ploy such as the 'renewed federalism' of May 1980!" the document declared. It stated that the best way to fight underhanded federal stratagems was to create an independent Quebec political force in the House of Commons. This would also allow Quebec's point of view to be put forward in English Canada. "One of the missions of the Bloc Québécois is to expose federal disinformation by speaking directly to English Canada."[2]

The Bloc also saw its presence in Ottawa as "an essential condition for the peaceful resolution of the Canadian crisis in the interests of Quebec and English Canada."[3] It saw itself as protection against any difficulties in the process of negotiating economic arrangements and Quebec's transition to sovereignty.[4] The Bloc's electoral victory was considered a necessity if an unequivocal message was to be sent to English Canada and the international community.[5]

The eight MPs divided up the various regions of Quebec in order to start recruiting and begin organizing the future party. Lapierre counted on the Liberals in his region, Plamondon recalls. "He called up the Liberal MNAs and the Liberal associations, and said, 'Call Bourassa, he'll tell you it's OK to set up the Bloc.' So it was the Liberals who set up the association, who organized it."

Elsewhere, in the ridings assigned to Duceppe and Tremblay, it was the Parti Québécois that was omnipresent. For his part, Plamondon, like Rocheleau, succeeded in bringing together people from both parties.

With a Little Help from Their Friends

When some supporters of former PQ leader Pierre Marc Johnson offered to help the Bloc, it was a sign that things were going well. The group of former Johnsonists was made up of friends who had met to discuss politics for several years. It included organizer Jean Fournier; former Montreal Citizens Movement director-general Jacques Aubry; PQ strategist Yvon Martineau; former Mouvement Québec director Nicole Boudrault; constitutional specialist Réal Forest; communications expert Yves Dupré, a partner at Sormany, Bazin, Dumas, Dupré; Isabelle Courville, chair of the PQ youth wing under Johnson; and Stéphane Le Bouyonnec.

This group found the Bloc's objectives interesting, and wondered how they could contribute. They decided to offer their services. A friend, Lucette Berger, was already active in the Bloc, heading the assembly organization. Isabelle Courville was also involved. She had known Bouchard since June 1990, when the Bloc leader approached her to take part in Forum-Québec.

In the end, Yvon Martineau made the first approach. He managed to arrange a meeting with Bouchard. After a few conversations, the group found itself spending two days in the Laurentians with Bouchard and his wife, Audrey. It offered the Bloc leader a ready-made organization, complete with organizer, communications specialist, strategic planner and so on.

They discussed the composition of the party executive, and decided to name Fournier as chief organizer and Courville as head of the legal commission. Le Bouyonnec would join the communications commission. Sylvain Laporte, another Pierre Marc Johnson supporter, would assist Fournier. Bouchard was interested, so the group was in and joined the founding convention, held in Tracy on June 15, 1991.

More than 900 people attended the rally. Of these, 145 were volunteers, 200 were observers, and 587 were riding delegates, each of whom had paid fifty dollars.[6] The composition of the audience was varied.

The media all remarked on the presence in the hall of former Péquistes, such as Isabelle Courville, but also present were the former head of the Quebec NDP, Jean-Paul Harney, former NDP vice-president Pierre Graveline, Laurier–Sainte-Marie NDP candidate Louise O'Neill, and Claude Rompré, Ed Broadbent's former Quebec adviser. Louis Duclos, a former federal Liberal MP, and Lyne Jacques, a supporter of Sheila Copps and activist with the federal Young Liberals, were also present. Claude Blouin, former president of the Quebec wing of the federal Liberals, was also there.

Several of these people would do more than simply attend. Claude Rompré would join the Bloc's policy commission. Louis Duclos would be the Bloc's principal spokesperson in the Quebec City region, regional coordinator for eastern Quebec, and a member of the executive. Isabelle Courville would head the legal commission, and Lyne Jacques would chair the youth forum until March 1994.

Some riding delegations were dominated entirely by Liberals. Plamondon remembers that Liberal MNA Jean-Guy Lemieux sent his entire executive, and paid for them all.

Nonetheless, most of the assembly was made up of Péquistes, and there was no shortage of big names: MNAs Louise Harel, Michel Bourdon, and François Beaulne, former cabinet ministers Yves Duhaime and Lucien Lessard, and party vice-president Bernard Landry.

According to Benoît Tremblay, one should have no illusions: the PQ always played a key role in the Bloc. "There is no doubt that, whether you are talking about the election in Laurier–Sainte-Marie, or the Bloc's fundraising drive, the vast majority of activists were PQ people, even if some Liberals were also present," he says. "You should not confuse different issues. It is one thing to telephone cabinet ministers to discuss specific questions, or to telephone Bourassa and his staff about specific questions. It is another thing to found a party." The Liberal presence was only really noticeable in specific ridings, and few riding presidents or candidates were Liberals.

The party statutes, manifesto and statement of vision were all adopted. The Bloc Québécois was on its way. The process had led to problems, however. Leblanc quit as caucus chair after the party was founded. "I've had enough of arguing," he told Bouchard. "Now I'm going to go back to my region and spend my time building up the organization in my ten ridings.

"It was a bitter struggle," Leblanc remembers.

Bouchard agrees. "It was very tough in the group ... Because Gérin, he wanted a party. So did Leblanc. And Benoît Tremblay. They wanted a party. It was a tense situation, very tense."

Gérin believes that the former Tories' insistence on forming a party, while Bouchard was hesitant, may explain his animosity towards them during the first two years. Gérin was well aware that Bouchard could not stand being pressured, and that his public campaign in the newspapers in early 1991 had earned him his leader's distrust.

He admits that he did absolutely everything he could to push Bouchard to form a party. Today he is satisfied with the results, even if he finds himself on the sidelines. "Even though it was more complicated than I expected, we have ended up where I thought we should go," Gérin says.

With the Tracy meeting over, the time had come to get organized. Bouchard was still wavering. He hated party affairs, and did not like having to deal with them. In fact, he would soon withdraw to work on his book.

An Arduous Start

The fall of 1991 saw the new party feeling its way forward. The party commissions were at work. The chair of the new policy commission, Yvan Loubier, had brought together an interesting group of individuals, including international law expert Daniel Turp, Ed Broadbent's former Quebec adviser Claude Rompré, René Lévesque's former chief of staff Martine Tremblay, and several people from the financial community.

The communications commission had been enlarged. Pierre-Paul Roy joined with Le Bouyonnec, Yves Dupré, former New Democrat Pierre Graveline and economist Pierre-Paul Proulx.

On the organizational side, people were at work, but things were moving slowly. The party had no staff and no budget. Everything was done by volunteers. "For quite a long time after Tracy things were relatively static, until people finally got it clear in their heads: we needed a *real* political party," says Le Bouyonnec. Despite the hesitation at the top, fifteen riding association executives were elected in November, and ten more in December. At the end of 1991, riding elections were being prepared for January in fourteen ridings, and for February in twenty-four more. Recruitment progressed slowly. At the beginning of January 1992, the Bloc had 12,300 members.[7]

In the fall, a fundraising drive had begun, with the aim of collecting $5,000 per riding. Plamondon remembers that the fund drive was "very difficult." From the Tracy meeting to the end of November 1991, no more than about $23,400 was collected. In December another push brought in $58,500. This pace was maintained, and by early January a total of $117,000 had been collected. Still, they were a long way from the planned objective of $375,000.[8]

The commissions and Fournier's team began work on a first detailed strategic plan to be ready by early January. The document proposed a communications strategy that would allow the Bloc to clarify its position on the political map and resolve a number of contradictions related to its role in Ottawa. In the long term it proposed the goal of electing 60 MPs. In the short term the plan proposed hiring four people, including a press agent for Bouchard. His assistant, Micheline Fortin, had been obliged to quit after the Tracy meeting because Bouchard could no longer afford to pay her salary. The strategic plan also proposed renting an office. Fournier felt that their meagre budget was sufficient to support a small office. Le Bouyonnec knew of some space that was available in Montreal's Place Ville Marie at a good price, because the former tenant had gone bankrupt.

The budget proposal and the plan were presented to Bouchard. Fournier and his group were careful. They knew that their leader was in a financially difficult situation and required certainties. "The risk had to be nil. It was a constant obsession; it came up in every discussion," Le Bouyonnec remembers. Since resigning as a minister, Bouchard had been strapped for funds. Only his book contract gave the Bloc leader some relief since the publisher provided in three payments a generous advance of $25,000.

Bouchard was tired of these personal constraints, and he did not want to go into debt. He was not thrilled with the idea of a series of fundraising activities. Who could say if it wasn't all a waste of time? If the referendum on sovereignty was held in the fall of 1992, as set out in legislation recommended by the Bélanger-Campeau Commission (Bill 150), and if the sovereignist side won, then the Bloc would lose its purpose.

Faced with Bouchard's hesitancy, Fournier and his team took care not to spook the leader. The budget was a modest one, and the money for it had already been collected. What would happen in six months when their little treasury was empty? Not to worry, they promised to find ways to fill it up again. Like the Bloc's MPs, it was now the turn of Fournier and his group to pressure Bouchard into making a commitment. "The push to build a party did not really come from Lucien Bouchard," says Le Bouyonnec. "It came from the pressure of people around him, including us."

At the beginning of 1992, Bouchard could see that progress had been made. He couldn't resist any more. He agreed that a more structured organization should be established. The machine was in place by mid-January. Bouchard also agreed to raise funds and take part in special events. He did not do so with any great enthusiasm.

"Starting a party means condemning yourself to raising funds," says Bouchard. "That was my nightmare. Fundraising — raising money to live on, travelling around, hiring staff. I had to hire people. That's expensive. Not a fortune, but it was still money we didn't have. So I had to raise money. I found that really hard."

For their part, the organizers and most of the MPs accelerated the process of establishing the riding associations. The watchword was diversify, go beyond the PQ. "We tried to control the situation," explains Le Bouyonnec. "We weren't against the Péquistes. We wanted PQ partisans and sympathizers, but we did not want the Bloc's apparatus in the regions to be swallowed up by the PQ machine. And we did a lot to attract Liberals, dissident Liberals."

Regional coordinators were named and documents drawn up. Fournier and Laporte held weekly meetings to stay on top of developments. The MPs played their roles, but to various degrees. Plamondon was among the most effective, but Lapierre wanted nothing to do with the process.

"I wasn't interested in the least," he says. "I did my job in the Commons, and that was more than enough; we didn't have any resources. And I took care of my network of Liberal contacts. I brought Lucien to suppers with people."

Gérin, who had pushed so hard for a party, was absent. "Gérin was not among those who did the most to set up this party," says Rocheleau.

"Gérin didn't deliver. Plamondon delivered, on the local level, everywhere," adds Lapierre, who was more than happy to see someone else deal with things. "When Plamondon organized something it worked, it was well organized. That work interested him more than the House."

As for Bouchard, his role was uneven since he was finishing his book. "He always had plenty of reasons for not actively contributing, but he didn't cause problems since, financially speaking, he was convinced," notes Le Bouyonnec.

A general council meeting was finally planned for Laval in June, to show sceptics that the Bloc was getting organized. By the time the meeting occurred, Fournier's team was content. Seventy-three riding associations were in place. Two remained to be created and elect their executives. The membership had doubled to 25,000. Party offices were open in Montreal and Quebec City. As planned, staff had been hired and the election organization was gradually being set up.

The Bloc's broad, nonpartisan image had been maintained, the leader was high in the polls, the membership had been diversified and the organization's leadership was different from that of the PQ.

Despite all this, a surprise was on the horizon. The Bloc's progress would be met with distrust.

Steering in One Direction

Some people suspected that the Bloc's creators really wanted to use the Bloc as a means of establishing a third option on the Quebec provincial scene. According to Bill 150, passed in 1991, the Bourassa government was obliged to hold a referendum on sovereignty by October 26, 1992, at the latest. If the sovereignty option won, the Bloc would no longer have a reason to exist. In this event, would the leader and his party simply pack up and go away? That would never happen, some observers argued. Within the Parti Québécois, there were many people who didn't believe anyone would be crazy enough to set up a political party for just six months. "You don't set up an organization while saying it won't exist in two years," said a Parizeau adviser.

Duceppe insists that the Bloc wanted to avoid conflict with the PQ, recognizing that it could be seen as a third option. And Bouchard admits he was afraid of antagonizing the provincial parties. "It would have been very disturbing to people in the PQ, or elsewhere, to know that we wanted to start a party that could be transferred to Quebec with a flick of the switch. Building a party meant having an organization and a fundraising structure, it meant having the means, the ability to enter the struggle." Bouchard maintains that "the Liberals were also afraid of a party that could move into Quebec." When Fournier's team doubled its efforts to give the Bloc an independent organization, by June 1992 the PQ's discomfort was palpable.

Parizeau's entourage had a second reason to keep an eye on the Bloc. Several of its members were close to former PQ leader Pierre Marc Johnson, who was also a friend of Bouchard. These Johnson supporters had held strategic positions in the PQ executive when sovereignty was struck from the party program and replaced by "national affirmation." Several — Le Bouyonnec and Courville, for example — had left the PQ when Jacques Parizeau and the orthodox sovereignists took over the leadership in 1988. Le Bouyonnec does not deny that his group dreamed of returning to the provincial arena, but he insists that this was a much more long-term plan. "It was clear we were working on the basis that the Bloc was an independent organization. The Bloc would play its role in Ottawa. Once the referendum was won, perhaps the Bloc might decide to return to the provincial scene. For us, it was clear that we were not in competition with the PQ before the referendum, but possibly afterwards at some point."

At first, the former Johnson supporters saw the Bloc as a means of broadening support for sovereignty, particularly among those people who would never support the PQ either in a referendum or in a provincial election.

"Fundamentally, no one was interested in working for a party in Ottawa," Le Bouyonnec continues. "It only made sense as part of an approach that said: this is worth doing because it will advance the cause of Quebec. Afterwards, once Quebec's cause is moving forward, well — it's in Quebec that things will be happening. So the idea of the Bloc as a third option was very much alive at that time. I would say it was the motivating force for most of the leaders of Lucien Bouchard's organization."

Le Bouyonnec admits that they were naive. They told themselves that "the stakes are so high for sovereignty that even if the Parti

Québécois did not like it, it could not take the risk of cutting itself off from a new source of sovereignty supporters." They were mistaken.

In Lapierre's eyes it was understandable that people were thinking of this third option, since they were talking about just a few months' presence on the federal scene. "We had to consider further action."

It is one thing to have thought about a third option. But, according to Benoît Tremblay, it was silly to think that it was possible. He is not bothered that some individuals gave their time to the Bloc with this aim in mind. "All the better for us; it helped us move forward." According to him, "you don't turn away people who want to get involved and who can contribute something."

Bouchard does not like discussing this period in the Bloc's history. He has lot of respect for the Fournier group, and he refuses to pillory them. One has to push to get him to talk about it at all. "I could tell that they were thinking about it, dreaming of it. The former Johnson supporters, people who didn't like Parizeau, who had had problems with him," he finally says, a hint of impatience in his voice.

Bouchard had always said that the Bloc would work on the federal scene and nowhere else. He felt the need to insist on this at the party's general council meeting in Laval on June 20, 1992. "It is certainly not our intention to define a program for governing, because the Bloc Québécois will never form a government, not in Ottawa and not in Quebec." He said that the upcoming referendum and election campaigns would be waged with allies from all sectors, including "our brothers and sisters in the Parti Québécois, and with their leader and indispensable ally, my friend, Jacques Parizeau."

When they heard this statement, Fournier and the rest of his group were caught short. Several had discussed what Bouchard would say the day before. On several occasions they had felt that Bouchard seemed uncomfortable, but there was nothing more specific. They did not understand why he had kept them in the dark and had not informed them of the position he would take.

Several party officials, in Montreal and in Ottawa, accused the Fournier group of hiding its intentions. Nonetheless, they all admit that they were sufficiently aware of what was going on to scoff at Fournier, Le Bouyonnec and the others on the floor of the general council in Laval.

Bouchard's declaration prompted the immediate departure of Le Bouyonnec and Laporte. They would go to the aid of Mario Dumont, leader of the new Parti de l'Action Démocratique du Québec, during the 1994 provincial elections. For a few weeks, Fournier attempted to salvage what he could. But he was deeply hurt that his support had been taken for granted and that the leadership had taken a position without informing him, the chief organizer, beforehand. Finally he left, as did Aubry.

Courville was already on her way out, however, giving as reasons a new position at Bell Canada and her pregnancy and imminent delivery. Lucette Berger and Yvon Martineau stayed on. Everyone who left did so discreetly to avoid alerting the media. They succeeded.

More than two years later, Le Bouyonnec remains convinced that Bouchard was trying to clean out the Bloc in order to satisfy the PQ, which was unhappy that Aubry, Courville, Fournier, Laporte and Le Bouyonnec were so close to the leader. "The environment around Bouchard was too Johnsonist," he says. He thinks that Bouchard was forced to choose between the PQ's support and keeping his little team of organizers.

In Nic Leblanc's opinion, Fournier and his group had worked to build the party structures, to recruit members and raise funds. He felt that they had a grudge against Parizeau, but not that they planned to set up a provincial party. His suspicions pointed elsewhere. "I always felt that it was more Lapierre who was mandated by Bourassa to develop a third option," he says. He emphasizes that only the Liberals could have benefited if the Bloc became active on the provincial scene. "With the sovereignists divided, the Liberals could hold on to power in Quebec. I think that's what Bourassa had in mind." Gérin more or less agrees.

Jean-Claude Rivest, with an air of sincere surprise, says that he never heard anything about this third option. According to him, it was clear that the Bloc was a federal party, and that the provincial Liberals would be fighting Jacques Parizeau.

The bloodletting did not stop with the loss of the former Johnsonists, however. After Fournier's team departed, Bouchard had to deal with another loss: that of Jean Lapierre. Bouchard, Duceppe and many others knew that Lapierre was thinking of leaving Ottawa. He was fed up with politics. He wanted to do other things and to get to know his children.

He also felt that he was defending a lost cause. In April he had been shocked to read an interview Bourassa had given to the French daily *Le Monde*. In the interview, the premier claimed that he was convinced that the constitutional negotiations, begun in March 1992, would result in federal offers that would allow the Quebec premier to avoid holding a referendum on sovereignty. Astonished, Lapierre sought clarification. He was told that Bourassa wanted an agreement so that the October 26 referendum, as specified by Bill 150, would be on new federal offers, not on sovereignty.

But there was surprise in all quarters when, on July 7, 1992 in Toronto, Constitutional Affairs Minister Joe Clark announced that an agreement had been reached in the talks. Bourassa's advisers acknowledged that the premier had to return to the bargaining table. For Lapierre, it was the end. After spending more than a year telling the Bloc that the Quebec premier would go ahead with a referendum on sovereignty, Lapierre had to withdraw. "I said that I would be available. If Bourassa decided to do something, I'd be there. If not, well, I had no intention of becoming a Créditiste of the sovereignty movement." He informed his colleagues of his position.

"From the moment Bourassa wouldn't go forward, I knew that the Bloc would inevitably become a branch of the PQ. It could no longer be a broad, nonpartisan coalition, since one of the two sides wasn't delivering on its promises. As far as I was concerned, it was my side, the people I represented, that wasn't delivering." He decided he no longer had a role to play. He hoped that the job offer he was awaiting from Montreal radio station CKAC would come through.

In early July, while Lapierre was on a family vacation with the Bouchards in the Magdalen Islands, CKAC confirmed the offer. It was too tempting to turn down: a three-year contract, an annual salary above $100,000, and a position as a radio host, something Lapierre had never tried. His notoriety had paid off.

Sitting across the picnic table from Bouchard, he wrote his letter of resignation. He warned a few people, including his friend Gilles Duceppe and his old mentor, federal Liberal André Ouellet, with whom he had kept in touch during his time with the Bloc. As for Bouchard, he was crushed.

Lapierre says that he tried, out of friendship, to persuade Bouchard to leave as well and to return to his law practice, rather than ending up as the "eternal opposition," as a "branch manager" or the leader of a modern-day Ralliement Créditiste. Would the Bloc have survived Bouchard's departure? Lapierre replies, "No, but that's all right."

A few weeks later, Bourassa returned to the negotiating table to attempt to smooth out the rough edges of the Toronto consensus. The final agreement, the Charlottetown Accord, was signed on August

28, 1992. The Meech Lake Accord seemed relatively innocuous compared to this one, which included an equal, elected senate with changed powers, recognition of native peoples' right to self-government, a guarantee that Quebec would hold 25 per cent of seats in the Commons, a promise from the federal government to withdraw from six exclusively provincial jurisdictions if the provinces so requested, and recognition of Quebec's distinct society, although with a restrictive definition and in the context of a broader Canada clause.

Unlike Lapierre, Rocheleau did not slam the door on the Bloc to protest Bourassa's decision to sign the Charlottetown Accord. He simply returned his Quebec Liberal Party membership card to the premier. Everyone had chosen his camp.

"Jean Lapierre felt obliged to make a choice between his political family and the Bloc. Staying in the Bloc would have meant a rupture of the worst kind, a battle," Bouchard explains with understanding.

Lapierre's departure shook the Bloc. "Who was the Bloc?" Plamondon asks. "It was Bouchard, then Lapierre and finally Duceppe. But in the Commons it was Lapierre [since] Bouchard was less visible because of the Bélanger-Campeau Commission and his book."

Divisions among the MPs surfaced again when the time came to choose a new house leader. Duceppe was the logical choice, but Tremblay and Leblanc opposed him. Bouchard turned to Plamondon. "You're the only one who gets along with everybody. Do this for me."

"OK, but after the election it's a different story," Plamondon replied. "I'll do it to give you a hand. But in the Commons I'll offer everybody opportunities to ask questions and make statements. I'm not trying to make a reputation. I want to try to keep the team together until the end."

The Impetus of Charlottetown

It was a difficult time for Bouchard. "At the same moment I lost my main organizer, Le Bouyonnec's team, which produced a lot of documents for us, and Lapierre, my house leader."

On returning to Montreal, Bouchard read an editorial by Gilles Lesage in *Le Devoir*. The piece was devastating. Lesage criticized the Bloc's lack of cohesion and concluded by wondering whether he should congratulate Lapierre for jumping ship. It was "a terrible, terrible editorial" that shook the Bloc leader.

With the referendum still pending, the tiny caucus met in Pierrette Venne's Ottawa office. The six MPs were looking at the newspapers, and most were reading Lesage's editorial. One of them pointed out another article, which assessed the forces in the field on the eve of the Charlottetown referendum.

According to Bouchard, on one side the article placed the major national parties, the provincial governments, the financial sector and so on. On the other side, was "a bunch of mediocre MPs, the Bloc Québécois," he recalls without pleasure. The group, extremely discouraged, tried to defend itself. "That's not fair; we are people, too." But they took the blow, and admitted there was some truth to the remarks.

"That was how the official forces lined up. [But] calling us 'mediocre MPs' was dirty. We didn't feel mediocre, but we appeared pretty damned mediocre and they let us know it. That was the worst time," Bouchard says. "Morale was at its lowest. We didn't have any money. I was always taking the bus. Things were really tough."

On the eve of the Charlottetown referendum the Bloc was without an organizer, and its machine was incomplete. The coffers were empty, and the group's four permanent staff were close to being let go. Caught short, Bouchard turned to Duceppe's people. He chose Pierre-Paul Roy as chief of staff and put Bob Dufour in charge of organization. It was Roy who insisted on Dufour. "We don't have any choice. Bob is prepared to do it, and he knows everyone in the PQ," Roy told Bouchard. Considering the control the PQ would have over the referendum machinery, Dufour's contacts were considered a necessity. Dufour had the advantage of knowing Jean Royer, special adviser to Parizeau and a member of the strategy committee. The two men had worked together for several years on Guy Chevrette's staff.

Bouchard could hope for only one thing: to participate in the No Committee and have the support of the PQ machine, which was the only organization that could make up for the Bloc's weaknesses.

Parizeau did not leave Bouchard languishing for long. He generously made the first move and surprised Bouchard with his flexibility. In August, the PQ leader left his Place Ville-Marie office and went to visit Bouchard, who was on the twenty-seventh floor of the same building. A friendly Parizeau shook hands with all the personnel, said hello to everyone, and then sat down with Bouchard. "I need you for the referendum." He expressed the hope that the two teams could collaborate closely. He told Bouchard that positions were open on the referendum committee and asked the Bloc leader to propose whomever he wanted from his staff to fill those positions. Bouchard gave him a list.

Roy, who quickly organized a small team of fifteen people to direct Bouchard's appearances and his press relations, would sit on the No side's strategy committee. Parizeau and Bouchard also agreed to name Louise Beaudoin, former Quebec delegate-general in Paris and today a minister in the Parizeau government, as secretary of the No Committee. Then Parizeau added, "You'll be vice-chair of the No Committee. You'll have a campaign tour, and a budget for it."

On August 26, the provincial premiers and the Native leaders went to Charlottetown to finalize the agreement in principle reached the week before. The same day, Parizeau and Bouchard appeared together at a political rally in Alma. It was the beginning of their fight against the Accord.

Their joint performance was a success. On the airplane returning to Montreal, they agreed that their two tours would meet a few times in regional centres, where they could repeat the experience. They also agreed to divide the work between them and maintain good communications between each other and between their teams. In other words, they agreed not to get in each other's way. The PQ leader would tour the major centres, covered by the national press, and Bouchard would tour the regions. It was clear that the opposite would be true during the federal elections. Bouchard was thrilled by the turn of events, since he believed he now had the means to teach Bourassa a lesson.

Once the Charlottetown referendum was announced, it would be organized by Ottawa in the nine Anglophone provinces and the territories. In Quebec it would be held under the provincial law that obliges anyone wishing to campaign to join either the Yes or No umbrella groups. The No Committee would bring together all the supporters of sovereignty. Many former members of the Bélanger-Campeau Commission moved back into action: Lucien Bouchard, Jean Campeau, CNTU president Gérald Larose, CEQ president Lorraine Pagé, and Union des Artistes president Serge Turgeon. The most striking development, because it increased the No Committee's credibility, was the creation of the Réseau des Libéraux pour le Non by dissident Liberals and its participation in the referendum committee.

When the campaign actually got underway, the basic strategy was, to a great extent, already decided, since the PQ had been working on it all summer. The Monday morning meetings of the No Committee, chaired by Jacques Parizeau, essentially confirmed this plan of action, but vigorously debated any new initiatives. Only the Liberals refused to take part in these meetings. In order not to lose them, the Committee agreed to provide a budget that would allow the dissident Liberals to wage their own campaign as they saw fit.

The PQ generally controlled the process in the ridings, although some Bloc MPs got involved. Plamondon, for example, used his knowledge of his region to recruit local business and religious leaders. The No Committee achieved some successes and was also favoured by events.

In September, the recording and leak of a telephone conversation between Bourassa's two main constitutional advisers had a devastating effect on the Yes side. After a temporary injunction and judicial proceedings had heightened the controversy, Quebecers learned that Diane Wilhelmy and André Tremblay believed Bourassa should not have signed such a disastrous agreement. "We were smashed, that's all," concluded Wilhelmy.[9] A bomb would have had less effect.

Next the Parti Québécois released the minutes of a speech given by André Tremblay to the Montreal section of the Quebec Chamber of Commerce. On top of characterizing Quebec's gains as purely administrative, he revealed that his boss, Robert Bourassa, had been exhausted and unable to express himself in English. "It is the Accord or independence," he continued, but no matter what the result of the referendum, either outcome meant trouble for Quebec.

Given the turn of events, Prime Minister Mulroney decided to act. Campaigning vigorously, despite his unpopularity, he arrived in Sherbrooke determined to catch the public imagination. In front of an audience he tore up a document listing "thirty-one gains for Quebec" to illustrate the consequences of a No vote. Although the event got coast-to-coast coverage, laughter was the only response from the No side.

Since the final text of the Charlottetown Accord had not yet been distributed widely, Bouchard and others began to joke that Mulroney had torn up the only copy. From the beginning of the campaign, the text of the Accord had appeared in several newspapers and was available from the federal government, but in Quebec it had been noticeable by its absence. The No Committee began accusing the provincial government of having something to hide.

At this point, Jacques Parizeau had the idea of having the No forces publish the Accord. The text would be printed on cheap paper and annotated extensively to show the criticisms and comments of its opponents. The No Committee would give the impression that it had been obliged to play the government's role in order to inform the public. The idea was a costly one and, therefore, risky, since the Quebec referendum law put strict limits on each side's expenditures. Several people disagreed with the scheme, but Bouchard was delighted. The two leaders' wishes won out. Thanks to the enthusiasm of the PQ's activists, some two million copies were finally distributed.

Then on October 26, 1992 the referendum was held and Canadian voters gave their verdict: No. For the Bloc, the campaign, and the No side's victory with 57 per cent of the vote, was a political lifeline. Defeat would have meant the end, or a slide into marginalization. "It was the 1992 referendum that got us moving again," states Bouchard.

"We had to win Charlottetown," says Duceppe. "After that, the sky's the limit." The referendum victory also meant that the Bloc had solved its financial problems. Shortly before the referendum the Bloc was almost penniless. The party could not borrow, since Bouchard was against it. The little money that remained was earmarked for the campaign, but at the same time there was the staff to pay. "The referendum budget, the No Committee budget, helped us a lot," says Bouchard, "since we transferred almost all our people to work for the No Committee, on the Committee's payroll. That kept us going until after the referendum."

The victory itself had other consequences. To begin with, on the positive side it pushed Bouchard and his team forward, encouraging them to finally complete their preparations for the federal election. Two days after the vote, Bouchard gave Roy and Dufour a formal mandate to prepare the party for the coming federal elections. Disagreements among the MPs would dissolve once the goal was clear.

"The No forces were victorious," says a party official, "so it was clear that sovereignists found themselves facing a process in three stages: the federal elections, the Quebec provincial election, and the referendum. That, obviously, pushed the party's 'on' button." Now it was up to Bouchard to take up the challenge.

The second result of the campaign was less pleasing for the Bloc leader. The victory of the No side confirmed that his dream of forming a broad coalition of Quebec sovereignists, irrespective of their provincial party affiliation, was dead. A few glimmers of this goal would remain, but the link with the PQ could only grow stronger. Bouchard, who has always refused to consider the Bloc as a branch of the PQ, recognized that Lapierre's departure and Bourassa's return to the constitutional bargaining table meant the end of the rainbow coalition. "It is true. A formal coalition including people who want to remain in the Liberal party and join the Bloc as well is no longer possible."

Rocheleau agrees. "The idea of a rainbow coalition was lost after Charlottetown. We had reached a certain limit. The people who should have joined us joined. That very fact helped strengthen the alliance with the PQ."

"It was right to wait, but after Charlottetown we had an election to win. To do that we needed a machine, and the machine that was the most prepared, the most dedicated, was the PQ membership," adds Plamondon.

"We didn't have thousands of people to win that election. We had key people in the ridings, organizers, but obviously it was the PQ who did most of the grassroots work," agrees Dufour.

According to Monière, this osmosis was not only inevitable, it was essential. "The two movements had to be coordinated, had to cooperate. There was no future for two distinct organizations, always faced with the possible danger of a conflict. A single logic was needed, a single approach. We had seen it before; whenever there was any discord, problems resulted."

Charlottetown was the first experience of cooperation between two parties, the concrete expression of the interconnection between them. The Bloc's hopes of creating a totally independent organization had disappeared, and the PQ was more than happy to fill the gap.

The 1993 Federal Election Campaign

After the No side won the Charlottetown referendum in the autumn of 1992, Bouchard was determined to throw himself into the federal field and lead the battle for Quebec sovereignty. But he had a lot on his plate. The press was sceptical of the Bloc Québécois and questioned the seriousness of a party that after a year and a half still lacked any conventional party structure.

And there were still PQ members who remained doubtful. "We knew at the time that there was a fringe of sovereignists who didn't agree at all with this. You have to remember that Monsieur Parizeau put all his authority in the balance when it came time to change the course," explains Pierre-Paul Roy. Parizeau did not hesitate to telephone the recalcitrant activists, ordering them to do their bit by handing over the party's list of members and donors to the Bloc Québécois.

The result? "We gave [the Bloc] the help they asked for. Those were [Parizeau's] instructions: whatever the Bloc asks for, to the extent that it is possible, you provide," says a close associate of the PQ leader. The Bloc didn't have the money to organize its own polls? At Bouchard's request, the PQ would add questions to its polls, done by Lepage. These requests were frequent and increased as the election approached. Each time the results were provided to the Bloc leader.

Bouchard refused loans and offers of financial help from the Parti Québécois. He did, however, accept staff sent by the PQ. From November 1992 to the spring of 1993, François Leblanc worked for the Bloc, but was paid by the PQ. Leblanc, who rapidly moved up to the position of deputy director-general in the Bloc, only became a Bloc employee in the spring, when the coffers began to fill up.

The Bloc Québécois had to work hard to stay ahead of events. Dufour, then party director, and Roy as chief of staff had no time to lose. Their offices at Place Ville-Marie were empty. The party had not held a general assembly in eighteen months. The coffers were empty, and Bouchard himself admitted that he had less than $100,000.[1] They estimated that the Bloc Québécois would need between $1 and $2 million for the federal election campaign that was predicted for the fall of 1993.[2]

Fortunately, Fournier, the former Bloc organizer, had managed to leave a foundation on which to build. The Bloc had associations and executives in all Quebec ridings and just over 24,000 members.[3] The party commissions were also active. But this was not enough. "The party was built by then but there wasn't really much organization," observed a party executive. The first decision taken was to set up an election commission under the direction of Dufour. Lucette Berger was put in charge of organization.[4] To mobilize members, it was decided to hold a general council on December 6, 1992, which would focus exclusively on party organization. The goal was to double membership and to raise $750,000 by the end of April.

The Bloc still lacked an official mechanism by which to nominate its candidates. Because time was pressing, the team borrowed from the Parti Québécois to draw up its own regulations. The Bloc regulations, however, differed in that they entitled supporters of a candidate to reside outside the riding in question. To encourage recruiting and thereby increase funding, the regulations also required riding associations to fulfil specific membership quotas if they wished to put forward their own candidate and not have one imposed by the executive.

The first candidate meetings took the party executive by surprise. On February 10, 1993 in the Ahuntsic riding, approximately 400 people gathered to acclaim the only candidate, Michel Daviault, former assistant to the Conservative MP Nicole Roy-Arcelin. The crowd was enthusiastic. So was Bouchard. "I promise you that the Bloc will be the federal party with the most MPs from Quebec," he assured his listeners.[5]

A month later, on March 7, 800 supporters from Laval-East nominated Maud Debien to run against Conservative Vincent Della Noce. Debien, a teacher and PQ activist since 1973, had been political attaché to the PQ MNA Jean-Paul Champagne between 1981 and 1985.[6] The same day, in Beauport-Montmorency-Orléans, about 1,500 people (of whom 1,183 were entitled to vote) gathered to elect Michel Guimond candidate. Former official agent to Conservative Charles DeBlois and a PQ activist for many years, Guimond defeated

Jean-François Simard by 631 votes to 552. Simard had been president of the young federal Liberals up until Chrétien's election as leader of the party.[7] In Longueuil on March 21, more than 300 people gathered, despite the rain, in the basement of the church of Saint-Pierre-Apôtre to renew Nic Leblanc's mandate.[8] On April 18, it was Bouchard's turn to gather supporters in Alma, and again there was a large crowd, approximately 600. Dufour was encouraged by the candidates' commitment and their diligence in selling memberships within the prescribed time frame.

Bouchard, who attended several meetings, spread the good news. In mid-February, he announced that, in a month, the party had raised $400,000 and recruited 13,000 new members for a total of approximately 40,000.[9] A month later, it was even higher, 50,000 members and about $500,000 in the till.[10] On March 21, membership had passed the 55,000 mark.[11] Seven days later, it was at 57,000.[12] On May 12, it was 75,000.[13] And by June 20, 80,000 memberships had been sold.[14] Dufour kept the registers. With money coming in, he could finally hire personnel. The office grew from two to a dozen, and during the election campaign the party had as many as a hundred on staff.

The Bloc Québécois still had a problem, however. The party had no star candidates. The top sovereignists preferred to wait for the provincial election, since power and a ministry offered more appeal than a seat in the opposition. The first people solicited were former PQ MNAs such as Yves Duhaime, Jérôme Proulx, Lucien Lessard, Adrien Ouellet, Michel Leduc and Laurent Lavigne. Only three agreed to run for nomination in their ridings. Two succeeded, Leduc and Lavigne, and only the latter was elected to Parliament. Over the course of the campaign, Michel Gauthier added his name to the list, when, at Bouchard's request, he stepped in at the last minute to replace a candidate forced to withdraw for having lied about his service record.

The second group targeted was women, who were known on the whole to be less favourable to sovereignty. The Bloc Québécois hoped to win their support with well-known women candidates. Monique Simard, former vice-president of the Confederation of National Trade Unions and television host, declined. She became a PQ candidate the following year but was defeated, only to be later elected vice-president of the Parti Québécois. Diane Lavallée, president of the Quebec Nurses Federation, also turned the Bloc invitation down, preferring to try her luck with the Parti Québécois. She too was defeated. Michèle Rouleau, president of the Quebec Native Women's Association, and Nycol Pageau-Goyette, former president of the Montreal Chamber of Commerce, both refused as well. The only one to take the plunge was Francine Lalonde, a former minister in René Lévesque's cabinet, who was eventually elected a Bloc MP in the riding of Mercier.

High-placed officials in union circles were reluctant to get their feet wet. Although tempted, Pierre Paquette, secretary general of the CNTU, ducked the invitation. Only Osvaldo Nunez, vice-president of the United Electrical Workers in Quebec from 1978 to 1992, threw his hat into the ring and won the nomination for the riding of Bourassa.

In some ridings, the party chose to leave the field open for local stars, but kept a close watch on operations. To prevent the possibility of ending up with a candidate who would switch political camps once elected, the recruiting team made sure all the candidates were convinced sovereignists. At Bouchard's request, Rocheleau agreed to run again, so as not to isolate Liberals in the party altogether after the departure of Jean Lapierre.

Not everything went smoothly when it came to choosing candidates. "We had people on the ground who took it all so seriously, they wanted to set themselves up as guardians for the Bloc Québécois. There were some really big hitches," remembers Bernard Landry. The malaise could be felt as early as March 7, when Michel Guimond was chosen as the candidate in Beauport–Montmorency–Orléans. That the gathering was a media success only left a bitter taste in the mouths of the party executive who had hoped to prove their movement was a kind of coalition of all sovereignists. Bouchard had favoured the former Liberal Simard. But the local PQ MNA, Jean Filion, had preferred to give his support to Guimond, and this had sown division in the ranks.[15]

It was during the race for nomination in Verchères that the real sparks began to fly. The president of the Bloc policy commission, Yvan Loubier, was invited both by the Bloc executive and Lucien Bouchard to become a candidate in this riding. But he had strong competition in Stéphane Bergeron, the policy assistant to the PQ MNA François Beaulne. The federal riding cut across two provincial ridings, Verchères and Bertrand, which meant that there were two PQ committees lined up behind Bergeron. Although Loubier's candidacy was supported by Parizeau, Landry and Jean Campeau, this played against him, labelling him an establishment candidate. The twenty-eight-year-old Bergeron easily carried the day, much to the consternation of Loubier, who had not foreseen the intensity of his opposition. He tried his luck again with more success in Saint-Hyacinthe.[16]

At the end of March, when a dozen candidates were chosen, the Parti Québécois's presence was palpable. With its 125 associations, each averaging 1,000 members, the Parti Québécois could easily crush the Bloc Québécois, which had only 50,000 members and a still embryonic organization.[17] In Joliette, despite a direct request from the PQ executive, the MNA Guy Chevrette refused to remain neutral and to let the Bloc Québécois do as they pleased. He favoured the election of his protégé René Laurin. Laurin was director of the L'Industrie school board, a founding member of the Parti Québécois and a convinced sovereignist. He was eventually chosen over Pierre Morin and Guy Amyot.[18] In Charlesbourg, the Parti Québécois were again divided. The former PQ minister Adrien Ouellette was set against Jean-Marc Jacob. Jacob was a veterinarian who had been very active in the Liberal organization of Marc-Yvan Côté, and for this he was severely reproached by the purist PQ activists. Jacob ultimately won the nomination.[19]

The worst crisis occurred in Mercier in the east of Montreal, which contained the three provincial ridings of Pointe-aux-Trembles, Lafontaine and Bourget. Two candidates had entered the lists, the former PQ minister Francine Lalonde and the journalist Roger Laporte. Laporte, who had been working the riding for some time, had the support of PQ MNAs Michel Bourdon and Louise Harel. At one point, he mistakenly thought he had Bouchard's support as well. Lalonde, the eventual winner, had the entire PQ and Bloc establishments behind her, from Bouchard and Parizeau through Landry, Chevrette, Garon, Boulerice, Blais and the others.

Although the Bloc regulations allowed recruiting members outside the riding, Laporte chose to concentrate his efforts in the riding itself. Lalonde, on the other hand, took advantage of the regulation and recruited everywhere she could. Her lead quickly became apparent. Bourdon considered the practice unacceptable and illegitimate, and sent a letter to Lalonde's supporters residing outside of Mercier inviting them not to use their right to vote, emphasizing that the Parti Québécois prohibited the practice of itinerant delegates.[20] Bourdon's letter was the last straw. "There are other ways of doing politics than those of the Parti Québécois!" thundered Bouchard.[21]

On April 2, Bouchard fired off a warning shot. "I have not spent three years in the desert building the Bloc Québécois just to see it turned into a fiefdom of local barons. If push comes to shove, I won't be wearing white gloves when I ensure PQ MNAs mind their own business."[22] The next day, Parizeau echoed Bouchard's words and called his troops to order. He did not want family squabbles between the party brothers. "We need quarrels like we need a hole in the head," he warned his party's national council. To the media, he maintained that his MNA Bourdon had "overstepped the boundaries. It's fine to question a practice. But for the love of God, let's not get carried away. Let's not put personal or local interests above the cause we have all put so much time into," he announced. Once Lalonde was chosen, Bouchard called for unity in their common cause — sovereignty. The PQ vice-president, Bernard Landry, for his part, asked PQ members not to interfere in Bloc affairs "when the Bloc leader has expressed such a clear preference."[23]

Landry feels that the selection of Bloc candidates turned out well in the end. He emphasized that in all of 125 PQ and 75 Bloc riding organizations, there had only been one or two serious blow-ups. And staff relations between the two parties were good. They gladly discussed strategy, communications, policy. When the election was called for September 8, the Bloc strategists overseeing the national campaign did not hesitate to call on PQ expertise.

Building Momentum

From May 16 to June 9, François Leblanc, Pierre-Paul Roy, Bob Dufour, Lucette Berger and the president of the policy commission, Yvan Loubier, shared the job of touring the regions in anticipation of the general council planned for June and at which it was hoped to draft an initial party program. From May 26 to mid-June, a series of regional events was held to raise funds and get things moving. In June, tension began to build. Bouchard no longer doubted that the principal opponents in the federal election would be Liberal since the Conservative activists were almost invisible on the ground.[24] So he set about attacking Chrétien, his favourite target. "Each time Quebec gets a good slap in the face, if you scratch a little, you'll find Jean Chrétien," he taunted.[25]

Chrétien was quick to respond. Campaigning in Edmonton, the Liberal leader accused Bouchard of desperate measures in resorting to insults, and then took a strip off the Bloc leader himself. "He is a separatist who betrayed Brian Mulroney. I always said that those guys don't like me and that I couldn't care less. Personally, I've always been a federalist and I've never betrayed anyone."[26] The insults went back and forth while Kim Campbell, newly elected on June 13 to the leadership of the Conservatives, launched her pre-election tour. She was shown giving speeches, doing the twist, kissing babies and cooking hamburgers with vacationers. Her popularity was rapidly climbing.

Throughout this period, the Bloc Québécois continued to elect candidates. On July 9, it needed only seventeen more to have a full slate. The last candidate meetings were planned for August or as soon as the election was called. And on August 14 and 15, with Pierrette Venne as chair, the first complete national caucus was held at Saint-Hyacinthe. The guest speaker, Jean Campeau, offered economic arguments in favour of sovereignty.

Although everything was going according to plan, right up to the end of June, the Bloc Québécois continued to encounter media scepticism. Journalists went out of their way to mention, in their reports on the Bloc's preparedness, that until June 1993, it didn't have anything resembling a platform. "The problem is that the BQ is a fragile, dependent party, with no platform of its own beyond contributing to conditions that would contribute to sovereignty," wrote *The Gazette* in its editorial of April 8, 1993. Right at the start of his report, *Le Devoir* journalist Michel Venne writes that "Lucien Bouchard unveiled the economic vision of his party, the one that was really lacking and which constituted its Achilles' heel." The recruiting of Bloc members also drew some questions, among them why some members were living in Ontario or in New Brunswick or why some could be a member of more than one riding association.[27] Duceppe accepted this as normal. "The objective facts were that we only performed so much [in the House], that we didn't have the right to speak. And Jean Lapierre had quit …" For his part, Dufour ignored the penpushers' gossip. "Each time, each time we set out a goal, we met it." He thought of it as a cake. When all the ingredients were mixed together, it was only a question of putting it in the oven to let it bake.

The Bloc people knew they had the wind in their sails. In June, they bettered their fundraising target. They had raised $777,000 despite the fact that they had been soliciting funds at the same time as the Parti Québécois.[28] They were equally successful in recruiting members. When the election was finally called, they had 90,000. By the close of the campaign, this number was 105,000. The party's confidence was shared by the Caisse Central Desjardins, which agreed on August 4 to grant a $1.45 million line of credit to the Bloc Québécois for its election campaign.[29] The financial institution accepted as guarantee the 50 per cent reimbursement of election expenses authorized by Elections Canada. Because the funds were usually returned to each candidate individually, the party arranged to have its candidates sign a form requesting Elections Canada to transmit the money directly to the party's official treasurer. However, to qualify for the reimbursement, each elected MP had to receive at least 15 per cent of the vote. And this remained a matter of faith, something the nationalist camp had in abundance.

The agreement was negotiated in July, although at first the financial institution insisted on a very tight schedule of repayment. Pulling a few strings from his days in Forum-Québec and on the Bélanger-Campeau Commission, on July 16 Bouchard phoned Claude Béland, the president of the Mouvement Desjardins, the Caisse's umbrella organization. On July 20, the Bloc's representative Michel Hébert advised his leader that the Caisse had become much more understanding. "Your telephone conversation with Claude Béland was certainly not unconnected to their flexibility," he wrote in his memo. The Caisse had taken a risk, but as promised by the polls, the Bloc Québécois did obtain the number of votes necessary and repaid its debt by September 1994.

Between Friends
The Bloc organizers had another card up their sleeves. They knew they were not without friends. "We really felt we had the support of the PQ machine," Dufour observed. The Parti Québécois had in fact been in the background since shortly after Charlottetown. As of January, the staff of both parties regularly exchanged memos, the Parti Québécois offering its expertise on numerous matters. They sent a three-page memo, for instance, on how to plan election advertising. The instructions were precise, detailed and professional. Dated January 27 and labelled "urgent," the PQ memo suggested creating a select committee of six or seven people within the following week. Bouchard made his own contribution by requesting that the PQ pollster Michel Lepage join them at least for their first meeting. This kind of cooperation was the norm across the board.

Whether Bouchard likes it or not, the result was that the party bureaucrats in both organizations came from the same mold. In a confidential interview, a Bloc official showed no hesitation in talking about his party as "the federal wing" of the PQ. "We are not talking about a nuclear family, but a blended family that works well," Bouchard's adviser remarked. "The network leaders, if I can put it that way, get along very well and are in close contact."

There is also no doubt that the two parties attract similar supporters, generally young and well educated, according to pollster Jean-Marc Léger. Employees from the public sector and the cooperative movement are overrepresented among supporters of both the Bloc and the PQ. Members of both parties are overwhelmingly Francophone.

According to a CBC poll taken in September 1993, 88 per cent of those who intended to vote for the Bloc also supported the PQ at the provincial level. Only 10 per cent were Quebec Liberal party supporters. The constitutional positions of supporters of the two sovereignist parties were also similar. About 15 per cent were sovereignists, pure and simple (15 per cent Bloc, 14 per cent PQ), some 54 per cent favoured sovereignty-association (53 per cent Bloc, 54 per cent PQ), and 26 per cent of supporters of both parties would support a transfer of powers from the federal to the provincial level.

After the election call, PQ director Pierre Boileau gave a hand whenever asked, and Parizeau's special adviser, Jean Royer, who never seemed to appear in party organigrams, was called on to solve special problems, which tended to come up rather frequently. And Parizeau's own chief of staff, Hubert Thibault, and his team of researchers were on the Bloc Québécois's payroll for the entire duration of the campaign helping to shore up the sovereignist cause. According to an adviser to the PQ leader, "Monsieur Bouchard said to Monsieur Parizeau, 'I need your people.' Parizeau said, 'I am happy to be of service to Bouchard.'" And like good soldiers, they handed over an entire organization ready to run. But, he added, the orders came from Bouchard, not Parizeau. The Bloc leader effectively kept control over everything, proving once again he had difficulty delegating. In the months preceding the election, all memos passed through his hands. He annotated, commented, suggested and decided.

The Bloc Québécois needed approximately $4.2 million to fight the election, including a little under $2 million for the national campaign and $2.2 million for its operations in the ridings. They drew up a detailed budget, but try as they might to massage the numbers, it was still difficult to do more with less.[30] They had just under $1 million in the party coffers, and although they knew they could count on the $1.45 million line of credit from the Mouvement Desjardins, they still needed more than $2 million.

A fundraising campaign was planned but nothing could get underway until the election was called. The Bloc Québécois still lacked official party status under election legislation, which meant that it needed fifty candidates on its slate before it could offer tax receipts to donors, an important incentive.

At the June 1993 general council, the members had set a fundraising target of $2.27 million. To fire everyone up, they had given themselves a tight time frame, only nineteen days — that is, the period between the issuing of the writs and general enumeration. The mailout to Bloc and PQ activists was sent immediately after the election was called, targeting about 225,000 supporters. The party hoped to collect an average of $31,000 per riding.[31]

The work was more difficult than expected, however, and the time frame had to be revised. In some areas, things rolled along quite smoothly. This was the case in La Prairie, Ahuntsic, Bourassa, Outremont, Saint-Denis and Trois-Rivières, despite friction between PQ and Bloc activists in this last riding.[32] In other ridings, such as Vaudreuil, the job was decidedly more difficult. In Laval-West and Verdun–Saint-Paul, several important PQ donors refused to finance a federal party. In Gatineau-LaLièvre, a Liberal stronghold, it was an uphill battle all the way. In Anjou–Rivière-des-Prairies, the list of PQ donors from the provincial riding of Lafontaine was in a sorry state. The Portneuf team was among the most unlucky. In addition to simply lacking experience, it came up against the weariness of donors, being solicited for the fifth time in one year. And the principal fundraiser in this riding had to be replaced after suffering an accident.

Some interesting information about the Bloc's membership emerged from this fundraising drive. When the Bloc decided to prepare its massive direct mail campaign, the PQ offered its help. The two parties agreed that individuals who were members of the PQ only would receive a letter from Jacques Parizeau, while those in the Bloc, whether or not they were PQ members, would get a letter from Lucien Bouchard. To see who should get what, the two parties had to compare lists. It was then that the Bloc discovered that between 60 and 65 per cent of its 105,000 members did not carry a PQ membership card. Both the Bloc and the PQ still make abundant use of these figures as proof of the Bloc's ability to attract a new wave of sovereignist support.

When it came to advertising, the Bloc Québécois was at a disadvantage. Federal election legislation required television stations to make available for purchase to the political parties 390 minutes of air time. To prevent any single party from buying up all the available air time, a broadcasting arbitrator was charged with its distribution. On August 4, 1993, the arbitrator, Peter Grant, announced that the Bloc Québécois, like other new parties, could only buy five minutes, while the Conservatives received 116 minutes, the Liberals, 78, and the NDP, 55. Grant had tried to smooth over the bumps, but without success. The new parties requested that the established ones voluntarily cede some of their privileged terrain. But none agreed.

As a result, the Bloc Québécois concentrated on making the best possible use of the four advertisements it had produced, all carrying the party's French slogan: *"On se donne le vrai pouvoir"* (We will have the real power). Organizers decided to count for the most part on the free air time allotted each party, and to choose their time slots carefully. While the Liberal Party ignored *La Petite Vie,* Quebec's most popular TV show, the Bloc Québécois used it for most of its advertising, which proved to the party's advantage. The Bloc Québécois also compensated for its dearth of television time by buying ad space on buses and producing large quantities of billboards and signs for balconies and lawns.

The party aimed its campaign primarily at those who had voted No in the Charlottetown referendum. Its media strategy targeted "Francophone adults between 18 and 49 years old who had some form of postsecondary education." According to a media plan elaborated for the party by Stratégem, this group constituted 40 per cent of the Bloc Québécois's supporters.[33]

On the ground, according to Plamondon, although the Bloc associations carried the ball, many PQ activists and organizers worked in the trenches. There was sometimes friction between the two party organizations. "There was a good working relationship at the leadership and regional levels, but on the ground we weren't respected as a separate party. Everyone wanted to have their own title, visibility, and personal glory," observed an MP. But in general, things ran quite smoothly. The smell of victory was too close for everyone to start bickering.

Bloc candidates generally managed to avoid any serious blunders, except Gilles Rocheleau, the candidate in Hull-Aylmer. On September 13, 1993, during his nomination meeting, which Bouchard attended, he maintained that the Liberal Senator, Pietro Rizzuto, had family ties with an alleged member of the Montreal mafia who has the same last name. The chief Liberal organizer in the province of Quebec, Rizzuto demanded an apology. Bouchard did, as well. Rocheleau complied at first, but changed his mind seven days later. On September 21, he held a press conference, told Rizzuto to "fuck off" and added more insults. Bouchard, furious, dissociated himself publicly from his candidate. The senator eventually took Rocheleau to court, asking $300,000 in personal damages and $100,000 in punitive damages. Rocheleau could go nowhere without being questioned about this affair. "I had to stay at home. That's what I did. I stayed at home. I campaigned from home." As a candidate in a Liberal bastion, he knew that he would lose.

Running Smoothly

Before the election was called, Conservatives, Liberals and many commentators predicted support for the Bloc Québécois would slip away, arguing that no Quebecers would vote for a party that would never form a government. The Bloc organizers ignored these predictions. They did not want their troops, so recently encouraged by the polls, to soften. Bouchard repeated everywhere that he aimed to win approximately fifty seats so as to carry sufficient weight in the Commons.

Aside from his goals to promote sovereignty, defend the interests of Quebec and to sensitize Canada to the cause of independence, Bouchard lacked a full-fledged platform. He launched his campaign with an attack on the federal system as the primary cause of increased fiscal debt, unemployment and wastage. He saw the regime as "ossified and lifeless. The present system is neither rational, profitable, nor reformable," he argued.[34] He advised Quebecers to "salvage what they could from the wreckage" in anticipation of their own day at the helm, and to elect MPs who would work for Quebec's interests in Ottawa and demand its due.

This was Bouchard's first actual campaign and he started out with a knot in his stomach. He feared that his party had peaked too soon in the polls and would lose the support it had gained, a fear he expressed repeatedly. As leader, his responsibilities were onerous. "We had chosen to give Monsieur Bouchard responsibility for the whole electoral campaign," a strategist explained. Although Bouchard had wanted to be relieved of some of his tasks, the Bloc team argued that his colleagues were not well-enough known. Halfway through the campaign, a SOM-*La Presse*-TVA poll showed moreover that less than a third of Quebec constituents were familiar with the Bloc candidates. And among Francophones, no more than a third could identify the Bloc candidate in their riding.[35] Bouchard himself admitted he did not know all his candidates well, and that he often did not know the local organizers at all.

His toughest challenge were press scrums. He was terrified of packs of reporters, just waiting for the chance to attack. "You're always tired, and over time the reporters have got to know you better and better, how you react, how to corner you better. And they're all in a team." Jacques Parizeau helped him out by touring the regions and meeting the local press, although few joint events were organized. The first, halfway through the campaign, was held in Shawinigan, the heart of the riding sought by Jean Chrétien. It started off well. Hundreds of supporters had gathered at the local CEGEP and the leaders were in good form. Warmed up by the cheering crowd, they started a full-blown attack against Chrétien. Parizeau accused him of having betrayed "not only René Lévesque but all Quebecers." Coming in second, Bouchard raised the tone. He added that Chrétien should try to get elected outside Québec, suggesting he was not a real Quebecer. Those comments drew the best answer from Jean Chrétien during the French debate and embarrassed Bouchard. "I am as much a Quebecer as you," said Chrétien, putting into question Bouchard's sense of democracy.

Apart from small incidents of this kind, however, the Bloc campaign ran like clockwork. Although unassuming at the start, Bouchard was in his stride by the second week when he visited Toronto, his only foray outside Quebec during the entire campaign. He held several meetings with the Toronto press and addressed the Empire Club. In response to concern expressed over the possibility of a minority government in which the Bloc Québécois would hold the balance of power, the Bloc leader tried to reassure the largely business audience that his political strategy was not directed against Canada, and that he had no intention of paralysing Parliament. His audience listened politely but was unconvinced.[36]

Two weeks into the campaign, an Angus Reid poll confirmed the earlier predictions made by politicians, the press and Environics: a minority government with the Bloc Québécois holding the balance of power. When the leaders were preparing for the television debates in early October, another polling firm, Compass, predicted that with only 51 per cent of the vote in Quebec, the Bloc Québécois could form the official opposition to a majority Liberal government.[37] Bouchard was himself surprised. His personnel immediately set to work researching precedents and devouring procedural manuals to discover what this would imply.

The Bloc leader, however, concentrated on the debates. As of late September, he scheduled regular intensive reading sessions, in which he dissected his opponents' platforms and worked his way through a mountain of information leaflets dealing primarily with the economy. Ever methodical, he annotated everything, added his own questions, and prepared himself for attacks. In addition to advice Bouchard received from his team of policy advisers under Hubert Thibault, Jean Royer added his own suggestions regarding the opening and closing speeches and overall strategy.[38]

The debates committee left nothing to chance. Their principal goals were straightforward: show the leader's mastery of the issues and highlight his image as a nice guy, someone close to the people and sensitive to their concerns. They were also worried about overly high expectations that might be built up regarding Bouchard's performance. "This is something we have to prevent," the committee communicated to Bouchard on September 22. They recommended "spin-doctoring" or influencing public opinion, starting to work immediately on the press on the Bloc campaign trail and on a number of influential commentators. Their pre-debate strategy was to suggest to the press that Jean Chrétien was a good debater, that Kim Campbell had the advantage of being prime minister, and that as a result the Bloc Québécois did not need a knockout to succeed, that its only goal was to get its message across. As a post-debate strategy, the party staff also insisted that Bloc supporters be included among the analysts on the special broadcasts following the debates.

Despite Bouchard's claims that he abhors anything resembling a communications expert, he valiantly followed his own experts' advice. On October 1, in Joliette, he put on a show of modesty, expressing his apprehension about the debates and having to face such "very tough and clever challengers," who would not be shy about making personal jabs.[39] He confided that he was the one with the most to lose in such confrontations.[40]

The night of the debates, October 3 and 4, he arrived with his wife Audrey, François Leblanc, Pierre-Paul Roy and Hubert Thibault, Parizeau's chief of staff on loan for the campaign. His "spin doctors" were Gilbert Charland and Louise Beaudoin. The debates were heated but there was no knockout. As anticipated, Bouchard made no effort to hide his sovereignist designs. He also repeated the necessity of reducing the deficit. Chrétien appeared calm and above the fray, whereas Kim Campbell was on the defensive, lashing out at every opportunity.

Neither Bouchard nor Campbell pulled any punches, but the prime minister lost in each exchange. During the French debate, she argued it unacceptable that sovereignists should run at the federal level. Mentioning René Lévesque, she claimed the place for a "separatist" was in Quebec, not Ottawa. Bouchard retorted that democratic procedure enabled Quebecers to choose their own representatives and that she would do well to leave the memory of his political idol out of the discussion. During the English debate, Bouchard put Campbell on the spot when he challenged her to reveal the actual amount of the federal deficit from the preceding year, and she was forced to admit she could not. In the end, however, no definitive victor emerged from the debates and the momentum of the campaign remained unchanged.

Throughout the campaign, the polls revealed a slow but steady growth in support for the Bloc Québécois, indicating that the party was generally successful in its appeal to those beyond sovereignist ranks, something which Bouchard observed himself.[41] Most Quebecers were untroubled by this revelation. According to an Ekos poll taken between September 24 and 28, half of Quebecers believed they could vote for the Bloc Québécois without supporting sovereignty.[42] In a SOM poll, the following reasons were given in order of priority for supporting the Bloc Québécois: sovereignty, the least bad party, defending Quebec's interests, a change, the leader, and, finally, the Bloc platform.[43]

Bloc staff, who regularly interviewed constituents from various regions, made the same observations in a report on October 1. "Support for the Bloc arises out of several factors: the leader's personality, the party's nationalist stance, but also a hostility to the old parties, a profound disillusionment that has led people to try something else. In short, there was a strong sentiment of frustration that favoured a new party, and the Bloc simply gathered the protest vote."

Bouchard played on this sentiment, and it resulted in a sometimes ambiguous message. In all his speeches, he promised to act as an advocate for sovereignty in Ottawa, but he also invited Quebecers, regardless of their views, to elect him to Parliament to defend Quebec's interests at the federal level. His opponents, however, pointed out the conflict between Bouchard's support for a sovereignist manifesto and his wish to appeal to the whole of his electorate. On October 11, at a supporters' brunch in Saint-Hubert, his approach suddenly shifted.[44] He seemed to fear that too much emphasis on the support of disgruntled federalists might call into question the legitimacy of his attempts to champion sovereignty in Ottawa. Bouchard instead encouraged federalists to look elsewhere. He argued that while they should be entitled to representation in Ottawa, this role should fall primarily to Liberal MPs. "I said that because, in the past, the sovereignist voice was never heard. It was unhealthy. It was undemocratic and I didn't like it. Just as I wouldn't like it that the federalist voice that exists in Quebec would not be heard in the House of Commons."

Despite the shift, his support continued to grow, and polls continued to confirm one after the other his future status as leader of the official opposition. Bouchard, aware of the annoyance this caused and preferring not to make waves, promised not to move into Stornoway, the official residence of the leader of the opposition. He also promised to be constructive in the House and to exhibit an unwavering respect for parliamentary rules.

It was clear that the continuing dissipation of Conservative support profited the Bloc Québécois most of all, with advocates of the *beau risque* now returning to the bosom of nationalism. On election night, October 25, the Bloc Québécois won almost half of all Quebec votes. With 54 seats, it was assured of being the official opposition. The Reform Party, having elected 52 MPs, came in close on the Bloc Québécois's heels. Liberals were elected in 177 ridings, enabling them to form a majority government. They won all but one seat in the Maritimes and Newfoundland and managed to do the same in Ontario. With nineteen MPs from Quebec, Jean Chrétien did better than expected. The real surprise was the loss of official party status for the Conservatives and New Democrats, the former reduced to two MPs and the latter to nine. These results were completely unexpected.

In Alma on October 25, Lucien Bouchard's tone was serious and formal. He was happy but concerned. Again invoking René Lévesque's memory, he said that the Bloc Québécois bore a "heavy responsibility — that of not letting the people down." He could not refrain from taking stock of events leading up to the 1993 election. "You would have to be blind not to see the domino effect. The No of May 1980 put Quebec in a position of weakness, and this led to the injustice of 1982, which the Meech Lake Accord was meant to repair. Its rejection gave birth to the Bélanger-Campeau Commission and the consensus that emerged from this collective reflection brought to light the real alternative then available to Quebec should the federal options fail — sovereignty. We now know what to call this federal failure: Charlottetown."

6

The Official Opposition

"Did you think about refusing the role of official opposition?"

"No, never."

"Honestly, were you hoping for it?"

"Yes. Oh, yes! But I was hoping for it the way I hope to win a million dollars in the lottery."

It was in the middle of the election campaign that Bouchard realized that forming the official opposition was a serious possibility. His aides had never dismissed the idea out of hand, listing it as one of the scenarios that could be envisaged. But what seemed to be the most credible scenario was a minority government with the Bloc holding the balance of power. This was the scenario being publicly touted all through the summer of 1993.

On October 2, the day before the first of the leaders' debates, the *Financial Post* COMPASS poll raised for the first time the possibility that the Bloc might form the official opposition. Bouchard was sceptical, and it was only at the end of the election campaign that he began to discuss this unforeseen scenario publicly. But on the evening of October 25, when the CBC announced that the Bloc would be the opposition, he forgot his scruples and was quite simply delighted.

"It was the next day, when I woke up, that it hit me. Official opposition? With whom?" He barely knew his candidates, but he was sure of one thing: most of them were inexperienced. And he was tormented by the question, "What would we do there?"

"There were all the conceptual contradictions. I have to say that the holidays were not a very happy time for me. I was very very preoccupied." He wondered how he would deal with the problems and worried about being shown up by the Reform Party with its detailed program and battle-hardened troops. He also feared that "we had landed one good shot and had nothing to follow it. We would suffer the humiliation of failing day by day." If he weren't a worrier by nature, Bouchard would have had no reason to be overly concerned, and he knew it. His staff had pored over procedural manuals, sent scores of memos and generally prepared the way for him.

In mid-campaign, when polls began to indicate that the Bloc could form the opposition, Bouchard's advisers went into overdrive. From October 9 on, there was one memo after another. Gilles Bonin, chair of the party's finance commission, floated the possibility of a research budget. Legal experts Charles Grenier and Henri Brun, who also had close PQ connections, examined "the practices and customs" prevailing in Ottawa. Jacques Parizeau's adviser, Jean Royer, was always on the scene, establishing a clear link between Grenier and Bouchard's office. On October 11, he sent the relevant pages of the rules of the House of Commons to Pierre-Paul Roy, who passed them on to Bouchard. One rule was a source of concern: the right to the title of official opposition went to "the group that, among the minority parties that are ready to replace a government that resigns, is the most numerous." The Bloc might fulfil the numerical criterion, but under no circumstances did it want to form a government.

Charles Grenier sent Jean Royer a legal opinion on October 15 to the effect that the numerical criterion had historically taken precedence. It was only when the party in question refused the role of opposition that this course was not followed. Thus reassured, Bouchard and his aides could begin their preparations.

Bouchard read everything that crossed his desk, and he acted on his advisers' suggestion that he decide early who would be the key players on his team. He would build the team around Gilles Duceppe and the new MP for Roberval, Michel Gauthier, who had been a PQ member of the Quebec National Assembly from 1981 to 1988. Duceppe was told on election night that he would be party whip, although to avoid hurt feelings, Bouchard waited until the next day to announce Duceppe's appointment and send him to Ottawa to get things ready. That same day, it was Gauthier's turn to find out that he would have the title of house leader; his appointment was made public on October 30.

The candidates were expected in Montreal on October 30 to do a post-mortem of the campaign and start up the parliamentary machine. "We worked mightily to appoint spokespeople, to make sure our members learned their lessons, to make sure they were careful. These were people who had never sat in any Parliament," Bouchard says. They wanted to avoid mistakes in renting offices and hiring staff. "We did a lot of coaching, we set up committees, we prepared policies and we really worked hard." Bouchard saw the situation as an exercise in crisis management: "We could have blown everything in the House; we could have fallen apart." The other danger he sensed was the attitude of the English-language press and an English Canada that "wouldn't let us get going, that would reject us, that would create insecurity, that would jam the whole thing."

The Bloc did everything it could to avoid irritating English Canada. Bouchard decided not to move into Stornoway, the official residence of the leader of the opposition. Unlike the Reform Party, which dreamed of changing everything, the Bloc committed itself to respecting the rules of Parliament to the letter and accommodating itself to the imperatives of the institution. To help satisfy people who objected to having their tax money go to finance the separatists, the Bloc limited office renovations to an absolute minimum.

With the new session of Parliament coming up, Bouchard's doubts extended to himself, for his caucus's lack of experience in Parliament was matched by his own in the role of leader. He knew nothing about procedure, he had asked only a few questions in three years, and as a minister he had learned only to answer when someone asked him a question and to stand up when he was told to. "Those years of infighting within the Bloc, when we were in the back by the curtain, we weren't there even if we were," Bouchard says. He didn't feel ready.

His first meetings with his caucus reassured him somewhat. While the Bloc members were not visionaries, he realized, they were sensible, reasonable people who knew how to express themselves and cared about the interests of their communities. He discovered that some of them had particular talents, which he refused to identify publicly for fear of arousing jealousy. He also realized that these people had entered politics out of conviction, not ambition. They didn't dream about pensions, cabinet posts, careers. With time he discovered that "there was a quality in their motivation that indicated other qualities in these individuals." And this quality had the benefit of being a unifying force in the group.

Who Am I?

Bouchard was surrounded with a team of MPs made up essentially of parliamentary neophytes. Five of the Bloc's members in the old Parliament were reelected: Gilles Duceppe, Benoît Tremblay, Nic Leblanc, Louis Plamondon and Pierrette Venne. Apart from these five, only Michel Gauthier and Laurent Lavigne, the MNA for Beauharnois-Salaberry, had ever sat in a legislature. Francine

Lalonde, who was elected in Mercier riding, was minister of the status of women in René Lévesque's cabinet in 1985 and a candidate for the PQ leadership that same year, but she never succeeded in getting elected to the National Assembly.

In contrast to this meagre parliamentary experience, nationalist connections are almost universal in the caucus. In general, Bloc MPs have impeccable sovereignist pedigrees. In fact, at least thirty-seven of the fifty-four Bloc members elected on October 25, 1993 had close ties with the Parti Québécois, and a number of them had been PQ members since the party was founded. Three — Antoine Dubé (Lévis), Réal Ménard (Hochelaga-Maisonneuve) and Yves Rocheleau (Trois-Rivières) — ran for the Parti Nationaliste in 1984 in the constituencies they now represent. Maurice Dumas (Argenteuil-Papineau) ran for the Rassemblement pour l'Indépendance Nationale in Terrebonne riding in the 1966 Quebec election and for the PQ in Argenteuil in 1981. Maurice Bernier, elected in Mégantic-Compton-Stanstead, was a PQ candidate in 1985.

Only nine of the Bloc MPs had no previous federal or provincial political allegiance. Three had a Liberal past: Michel Bellehumeur (Berthier-Montcalm), Jean-Marc Jacob (Charlesbourg) and Jean-Paul Marchand (Quebec East). Marchand, a Franco-Ontarian from Penetanguishene, worked for the federal minister of agriculture, Eugene Whelan, from 1976 to 1979. Three former New Democrats were Bloc candidates, but none of them was elected. Some had been prominent Bloc activists before the election, notably Yvan Loubier, elected in Saint-Hyacinthe–Bagot, who was chair of the policy commission and sat on the party steering committee. Madeleine Dalphond-Guiral, elected in Laval Centre, was not an unknown either. She was the regional coordinators' representative on the steering committee. A number of new MPs — Paul Crête, Christiane Gagnon, Monique Guay and Michel Daviault — had sat on constituency executives or acted as regional secretaries in the spring of 1993. Daviault, elected in Ahuntsic, is close to Duceppe. He acted as Duceppe's assistant during the pre-election fundraising campaign and would head the next such campaign.

A wide variety of occupations are represented in the Bloc caucus. As in the PQ, teachers are a strong presence: more than a dozen. Next come administrators, and then counsellors of all kinds, businesspeople, lawyers, and trade union staff members, followed by the three PQ political attachés, two civil servants, two notaries, and finally ten or so representing miscellaneous occupations. There are eight women in the caucus and one representative of cultural communities: Osvaldo Nunez, a trade union staff member who comes from Chile. The average age at the time of the election was forty-seven. Eight Bloc MPs were under thirty-five, with the youngest being Pierre Brien, elected MP for Témiscamingue at the age of twenty-three. Six were over fifty-five. The oldest was Maurice Dumas, a sixty-six-year-old retired teacher.

With no cabinet positions to offer or power to take away, the caucus avoided dividing into cliques during the first eighteen months. But Bouchard's advisers have acknowledged that there are some rising stars. Suzanne Tremblay, the member for Rimouski-Témis-couata, has attracted considerable media attention with her frankness and her theatrical performances in the House when she goes after Canadian Heritage Minister Michel Dupuy. Sources within the party indicate that the work of a number of caucus members has been noted, but one in particular seems to have attracted Bouchard's attention: young Pierre Brien. He made an initial impression when he delivered his maiden speech in the House smoothly and without using notes. Brien is intelligent and has slowly gained a position within the leader's circle of advisers. When the party's general council met in December 1994, he was always a step behind Bouchard, and he participated in all of the closed-door meetings that preceded the leader's speeches. Brien is also chair of the caucus's referendum committee.

Louis Plamondon has continued to play a special role in the group. Until the fall of 1994 he had no shadow cabinet portfolio, and so he had time to devote to his new colleagues. He had asked to be relieved of all his duties in the spring of 1993 after being charged with soliciting the services of a prostitute. The woman in question turned out to be working for the police. Initially, Plamondon pleaded not guilty. Then in early April 1994, he changed his plea to guilty, saying he wanted to bring the matter to a close. On April 6, the court gave him an absolute discharge, which means that he will not have a criminal record. The judge took this action because she did not approve of police officers trapping citizens in this way.[1] While this was going on and he had no specific responsibilities, Plamondon took charge of encouraging the new MPs. When a Bloc MP made his or her maiden speech, he assembled whatever caucus members were around in the antechambers and brought them in to hear and applaud their colleague. The fact that Plamondon does not hold a position of authority has helped him gain the trust of his colleagues and made it easier for them to confide in him. He also spurs the caucus's team spirit, which is important for many of its members, especially those who are not in the limelight.

Few MPs have had a chance to make an impact. Bouchard is at the centre of everything. He maintains a high profile in the House, dominating not only question period, as one would expect from the leader of the opposition, but also contact with the media. On a day when Bouchard gives a scrum, it is very rare for another Bloc MP to do so as well. Michel Gauthier is the only MP who ever asks as many questions as Bouchard or more, while Gilles Duceppe is very active in communicating with reporters. In the first five months, Bouchard asked sixty-six series of questions, while Gauthier asked sixty. Even without a major shadow cabinet portfolio, Duceppe intervened during question period thirty-four times.

By contrast, Claude Bachand asked only twenty questions, even though the Collège Militaire Royal in Saint-Jean, which the government has threatened to close, is in his riding. Francine Lalonde, the Bloc's human resources critic, asked only thirty-two questions, although the reform of social programs has been a major public issue. Finance critic Yvan Loubier, whose portfolio made him the Bloc's chief spokesperson on Finance Minister Paul Martin's budget, asked thirty-seven. And Suzanne Tremblay, whose territory comprises culture and Francophones outside Quebec, asked thirty-three.

Bouchard is the chief strategist and the entire strategy is focused on him. While he might like being leader, Bouchard does not like to delegate. Meticulous, hard-working, disciplined and rigorous, he expects the same of his staff. He is extremely demanding. When he is unsatisfied, he lets it be known. He is irascible and explodes easily. He tends to take some people for granted so that he permits himself more readily to tear a strip off them. This was the case with Duceppe, among others. Once he has someone in his sights, he will target his anger when he needs to let off steam. But Bouchard does not bear a grudge and readily laughs about it afterward. He is affable and informal with his staff.

Everything is run by a small group. First, there is his chief of staff, Gilbert Charland, who has been at his side only since the autumn of 1993. A history graduate, Charland is only thirty-six years old in 1995. He has, however, a long history of service for the PQ. Over ten years, he worked successively as a researcher, an official overseeing constitutional dossiers for MNA Jacques Brassard, a press attaché to Parizeau in the 1989 campaign, and finally an adviser to

Brassard. During the Charlottetown referendum campaign, he was part of the team responsible for the message of the No side.

He found himself in the Bloc Québécois by accident. During the election campaign, when the Bloc needed a press attaché, his name was suggested by Parizeau's lieutenants Hubert Thibault and Jean Royer.

The campaign over, Bouchard invited the workaholic Charland to join his staff. Surrounded mostly by organizers, the Bloc leader needed someone with a greater interest in policy. Before Charland's arrival, Bouchard had depended for almost three years on three people who had nothing in common with him other than their belief in sovereignty: Gilles Duceppe, Bob Dufour and Pierre-Paul Roy. After the election, they joined Charland in the inner circle, Roy as a special adviser for the leader, Duceppe as whip and Dufour as Duceppe's assistant. Pierre-Paul Roy, like his friends, got his first taste of politics within the student and union movements. He nevertheless has a very different personality from the other two. Small, discreet, decisive, this native of the Beauce region prefers to remain behind the scenes. He was the only member of the trio to have been arrested during the 1970 October Crisis. An educator at the Centre d'Acceuil Berthelet (today the Cité des Prairies), he was active in the union movement after 1973 and campaigned like Duceppe within the Workers' Communist Party from 1977 to 1982.

He climbed the ladder of the Fédération des Affaires Sociales (part of the Confederation of National Trade Unions) to become its vice-president from 1982 to 1986. In 1987, he made himself scarce, joining a friend in the Dominican Republic with whom he went into business. While passing through Quebec in 1990, he agreed to help Duceppe in his campaign, with the intention of returning to his island as soon as it was over. But like Dufour, he found himself caught up in the excitement and became Duceppe's assistant in Ottawa.

Bouchard quickly learned to depend on him for a number of tasks: sitting on the board of directors of Mouvement Québec, becoming a member of the supervisory committees of both the Tracy assembly and the party's communications commission, and finally participating in the preparation of all party general councils.

In the summer of 1992, he became Bouchard's first chief of staff, while continuing to supervise the Bloc's ties with the Parti Québécois and to support Dufour with overall organization. All at once he found himself in charge of the Bloc's campaign against the Charlottetown Accord.

Dufour, Duceppe and Roy carried a lot of weight, and at certain periods, controlled almost everything. During the 1993 election, Roy was chief of staff, Dufour, party director general, and Duceppe, responsible for fundraising. To run the operation of the opposition, Bouchard adds to the group his house leader Michel Gauthier and his special adviser to operations, François Leblanc. Leblanc was a former member of PQ staff who had moved on to the Bloc Québécois in the spring of 1993 to become the party's deputy director general. Actively involved in the party's operations, his abrasive attitude caused friction among the staff. In January 1995, Bouchard reduced his role and put him in charge of office operations under Charland's supervision.

"Power is increasingly concentrated in the hands of a few people," notes a party veteran. "It's even worse in the Bloc than it was in the Conservatives."

As a specialist in political communication, Denis Monière is concerned that no new personalities have emerged. He sees this as a major flaw: "The message is more effective when it's diversified. The more people you have with stature, a profile, credibility, the better the message carries. If you always have the same person talking, people get tired and don't listen as much. Having different faces allows the message to penetrate more deeply." Gilles Rocheleau, observing developments in the caucus from a distance, agrees. Familiar as he is with the problems caused by concentration of power and attention in the leader, he doesn't hesitate to give advice. "Deploy all your people, use all your people," he told Duceppe. "It's fun to be at the microphone, it's fun to be in front of the camera, but you should use all your people. It's still early." Monière makes the point even more strongly: "This is still the Bloc's weak point, because everything is too centralized or it all revolves around Monsieur Bouchard."

The Turn of the Screw

This concentration of power and visibility is the result of a disciplinary system that is the only one of its kind in Ottawa. Bouchard is so afraid of gaffes that the rules of behaviour he has imposed are very severe. Farcical behaviour, attacks on MPs from other parties, insulting replies and unprepared questions are formally banned in the House of Commons. Decorum has to be respected, and debates are supposed to be of a certain quality. The watchword is not to be provocative and to maintain a dignified tone. "I've worked very hard to smooth the rough edges," Bouchard explains, "and to make sure that they think of us as responsible people — to reassure them, in other words, by behaving correctly." There would be no more playing to the galleries the way Duceppe did in 1990 when he swore an oath to the people of Quebec after his oath of office to the queen.

"It takes an oath? We'll give you one," says one adviser. "This is what you want? We'll do it. We came here to make fundamental changes. We didn't come to make petty changes and we're not going to get tangled up in details." These are the lines along which Bloc members have agreed to behave. At the same time, however, they have worked out a meticulous disciplinary code — albeit an unwritten one — which the Bloc does not want to see appear in the newspapers. Everything is organized, structured, controlled, and the orders are repeated frequently. The first year, absences without cause in the House or in committees were not tolerated. In general, members had to be in Parliament four days a week during the first year. Duceppe keeps on their trail, making sure that they are in the House, attending a committee meeting or present for a vote. At the beginning, to make sure that all MPs got some experience, he insisted that they participate in the questions and comments that follow other MPs' speeches. He handed out speaking times himself for what is traditionally a free period.

MPs have to attend an information session before meeting a foreign delegation or going on a trip. When they come back, they have to submit a report. They have to refuse invitations from lobbyists and are not allowed to contact reporters without going through the press office.

With fifty-four MPs but only twenty shadow cabinet positions, a number of MPs were left without portfolios. After six months, with dissatisfaction beginning to be felt, the situation was corrected with the creation of a number of new associate critic positions. In committees, the leitmotiv is to respect the rules of the game, but in such a way as to gain as large a place as possible for the Bloc.

Members follow a busy schedule. On Tuesday nights, those in charge of committees spend two or three hours taking stock of upcoming issues, current debates and positions that should be taken. Regional caucuses get together the next morning at eight o'clock, with the full caucus meeting around nine. Every morning, the committee responsible for preparing question period meets to establish the day's priorities and assess suggestions from MPs. Chaired by house leader Michel Gauthier, the committee usually includes his assistant, Michel Bourque; Duceppe and his assistant; the leader's advisers, Gilbert Charland and Pierre-Paul Roy; and finally the head of the research bureau, Raynald Bernier, who used to be Bernard Landry's chief of staff. Once the day's themes are chosen, the research bureau checks the preambles to the members' questions and provides the information they need to make solid points. Then at one o'clock, it's time to rehearse the questions, make corrections, hear advice. The goal is to score points in the media.

At the beginning, few MPs were inclined to buck this rigorous routine. They were motivated and disciplined and wanted to do well. Even Bouchard's advisers were surprised at the amount of energy invested in the parliamentary grind. The model that Bouchard provided made the pill easier to swallow. He came to the meetings of regional caucuses and members in charge of committees and to the daily sessions to prepare question period. He gave advice freely, worked like everyone else and rehearsed his questions with the other members. He also made sure that all MPs could attend information sessions, participate in preparing questions and take part in debates on basic issues. In this way, everyone had an idea of the game plan and no one felt excluded. "He has a work style that brings about solidarity," one adviser says. By acting in this way, he acquired significant influence over his troops.

But within a few weeks, some members began to grumble at the control exercised by Duceppe and Gauthier and the scant visibility some of them were allowed. The new whip would light into his colleagues, swearing like a sailor as he demanded to know why they had missed a committee meeting. Those who had never been treated this way before were taken aback. At the beginning, one MP notes, this kind of treatment had a demoralizing effect, especially among backbenchers who had to content themselves with their constituency work. Duceppe also irritated a number of MPs by monopolizing almost all contact with the press, especially when reporters wanted to interview a less experienced or less prominent MP. "He doesn't allow anyone any visibility," says one of the original Bloc MPs. "He was always like that. He loves being at the microphone. Even now, he controls things completely."

A reporter who wants to speak to a MP is often referred back to the press office run by close associates of Duceppe, almost all former Rassemblement des Citoyens de Montréal (RCM) employees.

In addition, Duceppe keeps watch on MPs' personal behaviour. If he finds out that an MP behaved inappropriately in public, had one too many drinks or was vulgar, he gets involved — and not always gently. The control he exercises is unprecedented, says a veteran. "Nothing is allowed to pass," says someone who works closely with Duceppe. At one point, it went as far as surveillance of letters sent to party members. It's not surprising that some MPs found it difficult to adjust. Nic Leblanc noted that a number of them found the disciplinary regime hard to take. Things came to a head just before the Easter break in 1994. A bitch session for people to let off steam was absolutely necessary. After that, the reins were loosened a little. At the same time, the good reviews that the Bloc's work attracted calmed a number of critics. In Bouchard's office, it was acknowledged that the system could not have been maintained if the results had been bad.

In their own defence, the architects of this system argue that they were only trying to help the MPs gain confidence and avoid slipups. The only slipups in the first months of 1994 that have occurred have taken place outside Parliament. Bouchard's advisers identify at least three. First of all, MP Maurice Dumas was criticized for taking part in a public demonstration where smuggled cigarettes were sold in protest. Then Native affairs critic Claude Bachand had to be brought back into line after he went door to door in Kanesatake, near Oka, inquiring into the grievances of some of the Mohawk residents. Finally, MP Jean-Paul Marchand, who had taken up the cause of a Romanian couple who wanted to stay in Canada, had to be asked not to demand publicly that Quebec cabinet minister John Ciaccia intervene in the case.

The discipline Bouchard demanded had another purpose as well. He wanted his MPs to be ready for the second period, when they would work with a PQ government in Quebec City. He expected this period to be tense and difficult for his troops and he wanted them to be battle-tested and aware of their strengths and weaknesses as they entered "this crucial session, the most vital one." The troops had already had a chance to test their nerves. Human resources critic Francine Lalonde recalls the bitterness that surrounded the debate on cuts to unemployment insurance:

> The hostility in the House is obvious, it's clear, it's biting. You can't smile when the guy facing you says he's disgusted to sit in the same house with such an odious person as you. You react, but at the same time you say, "I can't let myself be manipulated; I can't let myself be pro-

voked." But the result is that a lot of us regularly have our nerves on edge and our hair standing on end. This climate has goaded everyone to work with increased zeal. Because of the hostile external environment, we've become a tighter, closer, more solid group.

Getting It Right

Benoît Tremblay notes that if, despite everything, the Bloc has been treated according to the rules, part of the reason is its status as the official opposition. If Reform had won more seats, he argues, the Bloc would would undoubtedly not have been as generously endowed with a research budget, as the rules for a third party are much less clear than they are for the opposition. As the official opposition, in addition to a substantial research budget, the Bloc has other benefits as well. It has the right to ask the first questions in the House. Its leader can reply to government speeches without being subject to a time limit. He has the right to a staff, enjoys the privilege of meeting foreign dignitaries and is paid a higher salary. Bloc MPs have priority in committees and are automatically members of parliamentary delegations.

Another advantage of the Bloc's official opposition status is a degree of political autonomy. It has its own territory, clearly distinct from that of the Parti Québécois, and can differentiate itself by taking positions on issues that are not traditionally discussed on the provincial scene. Being the official opposition means that it has to represent the views of all Canadians when it criticizes the government — as Prime Minister Chrétien did not hesitate to remind the Bloc just before the new session of Parliament began in January 1994.[2] At the same time, however, the Bloc was elected to promote the interests of Quebec first and foremost and to advance the cause of sovereignty.

While Bouchard did not hesitate to accept the position of leader of the opposition, some of the original Bloc members had doubts at the beginning. Nic Leblanc, who left a Canada-wide party to avoid regional tradeoffs and devote himself entirely to promoting the interests of Quebec, wonders how this role can be reconciled with that of official opposition for all Canadians. While acknowledging the advantages of the Bloc's new status, Leblanc says, "Still, it's harder. We have to be more careful. The other way, we would have been able to work only for Quebec, and it would have been easier." The Bloc can work in peace, without having to fight for things that are its due. However, Benoît Tremblay finds that the work of being the opposition is very consuming for Bloc MPs, making it difficult for them to work for long-term goals and concentrate their energies on their central objective, sovereignty.

This ambiguous position gave Bouchard headaches at the beginning. He is aware that it is an "incongruous" situation that makes sense only because it is temporary. But in this context, how was he supposed to reply to the speech from the throne? In December and early January, he racked his brains trying to find the right tone. The first versions he wrote were ethereal, with hardly a mention of sovereignty. A few days before he had to give his speech, he changed his mind: "I have no choice. It has to be clear."

Bouchard promised "our full cooperation to the good operation of the House of Commons," adding that the Bloc would "see to it, as far as we are concerned, that exchanges remain courteous though intense, rational though impassioned, orderly though vigorous." He immediately gave his fellow MPs a taste of what he meant. You could hear a pin drop in the House as Bouchard spoke for fifty minutes. In one broad sweep, he sketched the history of the last few years, put federalism on trial, called attention to the pitiful state of public finances, and put forth what in his view was the only solution: sovereignty.

> Let there be no mistake. Bloc members will not forget that their commitment to sovereignty constitutes the real reason for their presence in this House. One could say that as far as we are concerned, the prereferendum campaign has begun. Meanwhile, we will not let the recession be dissociated from its causes. For the time being, and until Quebecers have made their decision in a referendum, members of the Bloc will seek to safeguard the future by averting present evils to the best of their ability. These evils include unemployment, poverty, lack of budgetary restraint, undue duplication, threats to our social programs, fiscal inequity and loss of confidence in our political institutions and leaders.

In response to anyone who would cast doubt on the legitimacy of the Bloc's position, he added, "The universal character of these concerns confers a clear legitimacy on a common response to these issues. In addition, we received an electoral mandate."

After he had delivered the speech, he was satisfied: "It reassured our allies in the PQ, our sovereignist allies, the people who sent us here. And at the same time, for them [the people in the rest of the country], there was no more ambiguity. We had redeemed ourselves and we would talk about sovereignty when we needed to." In the days that followed, Bloc MPs kept on the trail that Bouchard had blazed. All their speeches were laced with references to Quebec sovereignty, past grievances and historical events. And as the months passed, the Bloc always kept its role as defender of Quebec on the front burner. When the Chrétien government cancelled the purchase of thirty-five EH-101 military helicopters, the Bloc supported the move while demanding that some of the money saved from the cancellation go to a program to convert military industries in Quebec to civilian production.

One of the first battles waged by the Bloc was over cigarette smuggling, which was especially prevalent in Quebec although it was occurring in Ontario as well. Day after day, Bloc members insisted that Ottawa lower taxes on tobacco products, as the Quebec government was demanding, to bring the legal price into line with the price of smuggled tobacco and thus remove the whole basis of the smugglers' trade. On February 8, 1994 the Chrétien government agreed, despite intense protests from the health sector and anti-tobacco groups and the opposition of eight provinces. The Ontario government was outraged and warned Ottawa that its measure would only encourage young people to smoke. The Bloc, meanwhile, claimed victory.[3]

When Finance Minister Paul Martin presented his budget in February 1994, the Bloc immediately attacked the closing of the Collège Militaire Royal in Saint-Jean, on the south shore of the St. Lawrence near Montreal. Another military college, Royal Roads in Victoria, B.C., was also closed, along with several bases. Bloc members were not against making substantial cuts in the defence budget, but they resisted closing the Collège Militaire Royal because it was the only French-language training centre for Canadian army officers. The government proposed to centralize its training activities at the Royal Military College in Kingston and promised to make the RMC bilingual, but this did not satisfy the Bloc. Again and again, it argued that the city of Kingston is inhospitable to French language and culture. The battle had symbolic overtones and dragged on for a year. Despite vigorous intervention on the part of the Bloc, the Saint-Jean college was finally closed as a French training centre for officers, as Ottawa had planned. The institution was taken over by the University of Sherbrooke and the Economic Council of Haut-Richelieu.

In the fall of 1994, the other noisy battle waged by the Bloc had to do with the cost of the 1992 referendum on the Charlottetown Accord in Quebec. Ottawa had overseen the referendum in the rest of the country while in Quebec, the provincial government had for political reasons held its own referendum under Quebec legislation. A week after the Parti Québécois won the Quebec election on September 12, the Chrétien government indicated that it would not agree to the Quebec government's request for reimbursement of a portion of the expenses incurred in the referendum. The Bloc cried foul, recalling that the previous government had made commitments and that Quebecers were paying twice, as Canadian taxpayers for the Canada-wide referendum and as Quebec taxpayers for their own.

On September 29, the government did an about-face and agreed to pay Quebec $34.5 million. It was forced into this turnaround by Conservative leader Jean Charest, who revealed that Prime Minister Chrétien was not telling the whole story. For days, Chrétien had been saying that he would pay if it could be proved that Ottawa had made a commitment to do so. On Wednesday, September 28, he said he still didn't have the confirmation he needed. The next day, Charest took advantage of question period to point out that Chrétien had spoken to Mulroney on Tuesday and had all the information he needed, implying that the prime minister had lied to the House. Embarrassed, the government issued a press release a few hours later saying it would pay the bill.

These high-profile media battles did not prevent the Bloc from also being concerned with issues of national interest that affect all Canadians: the reform of social programs, cuts in unemployment insurance, a replacement for the GST, international affairs. Lucien Bouchard maintains that he has not neglected either of his roles: "We have always tried to maintain a balance between Quebec issues and Canada-wide issues. Fortunately, issues that concern Canada as a whole also concern Quebec." He cites inflation, job creation and the deficit.[4]

The First Report Card

But the Bloc has focused almost all its attention on question period, the part of the House's work that enjoys the widest media coverage. From the time Parliament began sitting in mid-January 1994, the Bloc proved a skilful player of this media game. It was surprisingly dynamic. Its questions were sharp, its tone spirited but polite. On top of what was happening, Bouchard's team kept after the government. The media had copy every day.

Reform, by contrast, lacked bite. During the first six months, many of its questions were on subjects that aroused little interest. The decision of its leader, Preston Manning, to flout tradition and sit in the second row was greeted with derision, as was his proposal to put in writing a code of behaviour for his MPs. Meanwhile, the Liberals champed at the bit as the Bloc dominated Canada's public platforms. Bouchard's advisers believe that Reform's poor performance helped the Bloc. If Reform had done well, English Canada would have considered it the true opposition. In addition, as Bouchard noted in June 1994, "The advantage we had, I would say, is that expectations were not very high."

In private, Bouchard did not hide his happiness, saying he was "very pleased" or "very satisfied" with his MPs. He reported with pleasure how people he met in the course of his fundraising tours for the party told him that they were proud of the Bloc: "You're doing a damn good job." "You've done it with dignity." "We're proud of you because you've held your ground." "You've brought honour to us." The Bloc, and especially Bouchard, began to play a dominant role in the early days of the parliamentary session. Parizeau was elated. "The Bloc is doing exactly what we dreamed it would be able to do," he said when the session was a week old. "I would even say that I'm amazed by the extent to which it has succeeded in forty-eight hours."

On several occasions, it succeeded in putting cabinet ministers on the spot. First it was Solicitor General Herb Gray, whom the Bloc took to task for not intervening to put an end to cigarette smuggling. Then it was the turn of Defence Minister David Collenette for refusing to inquire into an incident in which shots were fired from an unknown source at a military helicopter that had landed at Kanesatake. Health Minister Diane Marleau was subjected to repeated questions about what she would do in response to the report of the Royal Commission on New Reproductive Technologies and about the tainted blood problem. The Bloc was so effective that English-language commentators began asking what the impact of its performance would be in Quebec and how prepared Chrétien was to deal with it.

The media all across Canada had to acknowledge that the Bloc had acquitted itself well. *Maclean's* referred to the Bloc's "polished, smartly driven performance in the House of Commons." In *La Presse*, Chantal Hébert wrote that the Liberals, despite months of preparation, "have quickly lost the initiative in the first parliamentary inning to the opposition, especially the Bloc Québécois." Peter O'Neil, writing in the Vancouver *Sun*, concluded that Reform MPs would have to work hard if they wanted to steal the limelight from the Bloc. And Toronto *Globe and Mail* columnist Giles Gherson wrote, "Parliament Hill veterans hate to say it, but they do anyway: they're impressed with the Bloc Québécois."[5]

7

The Backlash

Not everyone was happy with the Bloc's performance in the election and in the House. Its confirmation as the official opposition made waves outside Quebec. But English Canadian anxiety had begun to show up even before the Bloc's unexpected success in the election. According to a September 1993 poll, most Canadians believed that a strong Bloc presence in the House of Commons would be a threat to Canadian unity.[1]

The federalist political elite shared this opinion and expressed its apprehension. During visits to Quebec during the election campaign, Frank McKenna, the Liberal premier of New Brunswick, and David Peterson, the former Liberal premier of Ontario, evoked the negative consequences of a vote for the Bloc. Then it was Premier Robert Bourassa's turn to warn Quebecers of the risks of political destabilization. Ontario's NDP premier, Bob Rae, chimed in as well: "Let's not pussyfoot around about the words. [Bouchard] wants to break up Canada ... and he wants to kid everybody in saying this can be done without any expense and it can be done without any problem." Rae said he was not prepared to sit quietly by during the election while everyone called the Bloc a Quebec issue, when its constitutional option would have tremendous consequences for the rest of the country.[2]

And then there were the inflammatory comments. David Peterson touched off a controversy by saying on TV Ontario that while he didn't want to compare Bouchard to Hitler, the two men shared the characteristic of leading a movement based on a feeling of humiliation and rejection.[3] Conservative MP Bob Horner suggested that instead of being allowed to participate in the leaders' debate, Bouchard should be tried for treason. His leader, Kim Campbell, put forward the idea that the Bloc was attracting support because it was keeping its intentions a secret. Perhaps thinking that Quebecers are completely stupid, she said, "I think they [Quebec federalist voters] don't know that Mr. Bouchard's goal is the independence of Quebec." As a symbol of the sovereignist struggle, Bouchard was twice the object of threats, once during the election campaign and again after he had been elected in Ottawa.[4]

In January 1994 a Toronto investment consultant, Raymond Aaron, initiated a lawsuit in the name of all Canadians for $500 billion in damages against the fifty-four Bloc members. He maintained that $500 billion was the value of the losses incurred by the country after their election and the uncertainty created by their political program.[5]

Preston Manning, leader of the Reform Party, was visibly frustrated at seeing official opposition status slip through its fingers. He said it would play that role de facto because the Bloc only represented Quebec. Manning demanded offices equivalent to the Bloc's and rotation of the two opposition parties in asking the first question in the House. Bouchard was furious. Casting doubt on the results of a democratic exercise was incomprehensible to him. He told *Maclean's*:

> Who do those Reformers think they are? Either they are or they are not the official Opposition. If we had not become the official Opposition, we would not have demanded the right to ask the first question in Question Period. We wouldn't have tried to get better offices. I am the Leader of the Opposition and I will act as such. I will ask the first question. Every day.[6]

Bouchard and his advisers interpreted these extreme reactions as the product of a rude awakening: English Canadians had not seen the Bloc coming. As proof, they cite the fact that most Canada-wide polls underestimated the Bloc's strength in comparison with polls taken in Quebec alone. "Other Canadians got a false sense of security," says Daniel Turp, chair of the Bloc's policy commission. "That's why people were so surprised to see the Bloc elected, to see the Bloc with fifty-four seats and even official opposition status." Pollster Jean-Marc Léger came to the same conclusion:

> Canadian polling firms gave the Bloc Québécois about 20 per cent of the vote for two years, from the time the Bloc was formed to just before the election campaign. During the election campaign, all of a sudden, they climbed to 40 per cent of the vote. All of a sudden. Here in Quebec, we

were one of the only firms that said the Bloc always had
between 40 and 45 per cent of the vote. The conclusion
you can draw from this is that Quebecers expected the
election of the Bloc and a certain number of seats while
English Canadians didn't expect it at all.

According to Léger, English Canadians did not have time to assess
the impact of the Bloc's rise fully:

> It was only when Monsieur Bouchard made some state-
> ments outside Canada that they saw the consequences of
> the importance of having a leader of the opposition who
> came from Quebec and represented a sovereignist party.
> And that's when they suddenly started to raise a fuss. The
> fuss started six months later.

Building Bridges

Bouchard said he didn't want to make an enemy of English Canada.
When he established the Bloc, he did not limit its mandate to protecting the interests of Quebec. He also saw it as his mission to
become a messenger from Quebec to the rest of the country. "To you
who live in Toronto, Winnipeg, Calgary, Vancouver, Fredericton or
St. John's, and are trying to form an idea of the Bloc Québécois and
its mission," he said during the party's founding meeting, "I would
like to say that we are in Ottawa to tell you about today's Quebec."
More precisely, he wanted to make English Canada aware that sovereignty was coming so that it would be prepared to undertake the
negotiations that would follow an eventual separation. The Bloc
expects to play a watchdog role during these talks.

But this approach has its contradictions. It is questionable whether
Bouchard is courting English Canadians or whether he is really
courting Quebecers who are worried about what will happen after a
declaration of independence. Focus groups, which the party organ-
izes on occasion in Quebec, have indicated, according to a party
memo, that "people are very worried about what will happen to
Canada, how it will react and especially, once Quebec is sovereign,
what Canada will be able to do to survive."

Consequently, Bouchard has had a dual job: reassure Quebecers
and reassure the rest of Canada. As with his work in the House, in
meetings with Canadians and foreign representatives, Bouchard did
not want to leave anything to chance. As soon as the election was

over, he identified his targets. In English Canada, he concentrated on building bridges with the business community; with the English Canadian left, which appeared more receptive to his plans than other Canadians; and with intellectuals. His contacts with intellectuals, however, have been private and limited, as have most of his meetings with trade union representatives.

Whether he is in Ottawa or on tour, Bouchard sets aside time for closed-door meetings. In this way, he was able to have a relaxed exchange of views with the president of the Canadian Labour Congress, Bob White. He doesn't ask for meetings, but he accepts almost every one that is proposed to him. This was how he began his efforts to court the business community. In addition to giving speeches before audiences such as the Canadian Club and the Calgary Chamber of Commerce, he agreed to private exchanges with business leaders.

In May 1994, however, he put on the brakes after he saw reports in the press that in his view distorted remarks he had made before a Canadian Chamber of Commerce audience. According to Canadian Press, Bouchard said, among other things, that if Quebec became sovereign the United States would annex British Columbia and it was reasonable to fear that a large number of English Quebecers would leave the province. Bouchard immediately issued a press release to nuance his statements. Contrary to reports, he said he did not predict that the Bloc would obstruct the functioning of the House of Commons if the democratically expressed will of Quebecers was not respected. Rather, he had wondered aloud about the kind of country, the level of collective cohesion and the sort of Parliament there would be in light of the prevailing frustration. He also reiterated his conviction that the rest of Canada would form a country if Quebec became independent and that he was not afraid of an exodus of Anglophone Quebecers.

Bouchard was disappointed by this incident because he considered the business community very important. He believes that most businesspeople are pragmatists who see sovereignty as a problem to manage and overcome. He sees them as having the potential to make a difference in the aftermath of a Yes vote by putting pressure on the federal government to negotiate things that would be essential to maintaining their financial interests.

Bouchard does not rely only on organized groups. He also takes advantage of his network of contacts. One of his contacts is Peter White, an old university friend of Bouchard's who worked in Prime

Minister Mulroney's office before returning to the private sector as
the head of Unimédia. White invited Bouchard to a Canada-France
business relations club meeting in Cambridge, Ontario. He also in-
troduced the Bloc leader to the disputatious Montreal writer, Mordecai Richler. Accompanied by their wives, White, Bouchard and
Richler had dinner in a room at the Ritz-Carlton Hotel in Montreal.
Bouchard reports having enjoyed the evening greatly: "Mordecai is
a funny guy. We laughed like crazy. We had fun. Oh, yes ..."

Bouchard prefers his contacts with intellectuals: "Communication
is more direct. People say things." He is counting on intellectuals to
be "catalysts of rationality" in the wider public. He believes English
Canada will have no choice:

> After they've said all sorts of things, after they've gotten
> angry, if Quebecers say yes to sovereignty, that counts for
> a lot, they will have no choice ... And when they've
> realized that they have no choice, they will have to do
> some common-sense things to protect their own interests.
> Because then, their own interest will be a mutual interest
> in having a transition that won't be too harsh from an
> economic point of view.

For Bouchard, that means they will continue to do business.

Bouchard has another concern: international recognition of a sovereign Quebec. He has established goals and priority targets — the
United States and France. In the case of the United States, he is
convinced that the Americans can have a stabilizing effect on the
Canadian government, as they would try to protect their economic
interests. It was former French prime minister Michel Rocard who
aroused Bouchard's interest in the United States when he came to
Quebec to observe the twenty-fifth anniversary of the Parti
Québécois in August 1993. During a supper in his honour, Rocard
gave Bouchard some advice: "You sovereignists, you count too much
on France. Don't forget the United States — it will be a trump card
in the game, for you and for us." Bouchard paid attention. His first
foreign trip as opposition leader would be to the United States. At
the same time, he retains his unquenchable affection for France, and
that would be the destination of his second foreign trip.

In Canada, he takes advantage of his status as opposition leader
to establish and cultivate ties with foreign diplomats. After he arrived
in Ottawa for the opening of the parliamentary session in January

1994, he met with diplomats at a rate of about two per week. Some of these meetings were requested by the embassies in question: the French, British, American, German and Mexican embassies were among those that initiated meetings. The Bloc also decided to participate in parliamentary delegations to foreign countries. It had several goals in mind: visibility, an opportunity to answer questions, a reminder that a democratic process is involved, preparation of hearts and minds, and cultivation of friendships that could be useful in the future.

In taking the Bloc's message to the rest of Canada and other countries, Bouchard is the most prominent actor, but other Bloc MPs also have to play their parts as spokespeople, representatives on committees or members of parliamentary delegations. At the beginning, their activities in these roles were tightly controlled. Before visiting another province, the MPs would be given information about its political situation and local concerns. They were given instructions in answering questions about language laws or accusations of fascism or treason and warned about the prejudices of the local press. When they came back, they had to submit a report so that the Bloc could reflect on the experience and fine-tune its positions.

Some MPs used their positions in the shadow cabinet to open some doors at home. Human resources critic Francine Lalonde established contacts with grassroots and trade-union movements. Finance critic Yvan Loubier formed similar ties with the business community, which he found considerably more proactive than other groups. Bond rating agencies, brokerage firms and economic advisers in embassies made contact with him to find out about what the sovereignist camp would do after a referendum. But there was a surprise for Loubier in these meetings. He found out that people in the business community were not familiar with the modalities when one sovereign state succeeds another, especially as regards trade agreements.

Fixing Fences

Winning the confidence of Canadians has not always been easy, especially since over the years Bouchard himself has made inflammatory statements. When minority government scenarios were in the air in December 1992, he said, "This minority government, we'll make it dance." The next month, PQ leader Jacques Parizeau fanned the flames by promising that there would be "an Italian-style parliament" and "the weakest government in our history."[7] Challenged on these statements, Bouchard tried to repair the damage by repeating that Quebecers did not want a "disorderly government in Ottawa." But doubts did not go away, and the statements would often come back to haunt him.

In April 1993, at his nomination meeting in Alma, Bouchard regressed again: "Quebecers have always been told that the English understand finance, that financial matters should be left to them. Well, we've let them run Canada and now they've brought the country to the brink of bankruptcy." The next day, the Montreal *Gazette* reacted. Its columnist, Don Macpherson, reminded Bouchard that many Francophones, notably Pierre Trudeau, had contributed to running the country. "The worst thing about Bouchard's remark is not that it is a lie," he wrote. "It is that it is a racist lie. And it makes the political leader who uttered it appear to be a hypocrite as well as a demagogue."[8]

The distinction between "us" and "them" surfaced again during the training session for Bloc candidates in mid-August and in the interviews that followed. "If they [the rest of Canada] are intent on going bankrupt, let them go," Bouchard said. "But we're going to save our skin."[9] "Saving our skin" was a constant theme, along with *"sauver les meubles"* (saving the furniture) and "limiting the damage."

During the election campaign, confusion about Bouchard's intentions persisted. Visiting the offices of the Toronto *Star*, he maintained that if he had the balance of power, he would have "raw power" that he could use if the interests of Quebec were in question.[10] However, speaking to the Canadian Club the same day, he said that "it is not the Bloc Québécois's intention to paralyze the House of Commons." On October 6, in Quebec City, Bouchard was still sending out mixed signals. "We will invade the House of Commons," he said in an antagonistic tone. "Quebec will stand upright in front of Canada. People in Toronto will lie awake at night."[11] But when English Canada's nervousness was reported to him, he replied, "It has to be said that we haven't adequately explained our problems to the rest of Canada. Most of us have stayed pretty far away."

As the possibility of forming the official opposition loomed larger, he increasingly sought to smooth the rough edges and emphasize the common interests of Canadians and Quebecers. His tone became more statesmanlike. On election night, he felt that he had to go a step further:

Our plan to become sovereign is not directed against Canada. It represents a rejection of unproductive quarrels and navel-gazing conflicts. Most of all, it is the only adequate response to the challenges issued to us by a world that is changing profoundly ... I say to our friends in English Canada that our victory tonight represents a unique opportunity to establish a new relationship based on truth and respect ... We are going to Ottawa to build something new, something that will prove positive for both nations of Canada.

Two weeks later, after swearing his oath to the queen, Bouchard continued along the same lines: "I see being the official opposition through the prism of equity. Equity is for everyone: for Quebec, but also for Canada as a whole. Until Quebecers decide to change their political institutions, we are part of a federation that treats people with equity."[12] To prove his point while advancing its cause, the Bloc has been careful in choosing the subjects on which to intervene in the House of Commons. The House is still its best channel for communicating with the population as a whole. All the national media are represented there, and they ensure that there is follow-up, which makes it easier for the Bloc to disseminate its message.

The key to good media coverage is playing the parliamentary game skilfully, which the Bloc has done. The clearest case has been its defence of the Canadian ownership of Ginn Publishing. The Liberal government authorized the return of 51 per cent of the shares of the textbook publisher to its original owner, the American giant Paramount Communications, for $10.3 million. Heritage Minister Michel Dupuy gave his consent because he believed that he was bound by a three-year-old legal opinion. The problem was that the legal opinion was questionable and Dupuy had reportedly not read it.[13]

Setting itself up as the defender of Canadian culture, the Bloc questioned the government about the Ginn affair day after day in mid-March, almost always in English. It even devoted an opposition day to the affair.[14] English Canadian journalists were surprised. The issue slowly caught on, and it made the front page of a number of major newspapers. Bouchard's advisers were proud of the "coup" they had achieved. They wanted to show Canadians that they could be Canadian nationalists defending Canadian culture, and that this was acceptable. They succeeded. Showing Canadians the positive aspect of their own nationalism, the calculation went, would help them recognize the positive aspect of Quebec nationalism as well.

The Bloc elicited the same surprised reaction when it supported the continuation of Cruise missile tests over Canadian territory. Given the makeup of the Bloc caucus, observers had expected it to oppose Cruise missile testing, but it didn't. This decision was not an easy one. "It was controversial because a lot of people in the Bloc didn't agree with continuing the tests," Bouchard explains. "But there were strategic considerations involved." The "strategic consideration" was Bouchard's planned trip to Washington in the coming weeks. "Because this was coming up so soon and the message we had to get across to our powerful American neighbour was so important," one adviser explains "we quickly came to a consensus" on the position. Such are the constraints that go along with trying to get the ear of the powerful.

Bouchard's first visit to Washington and New York in 1994 did not provoke the expected outcry, even though he took a side trip to the United Nations, where he spoke with Secretary General Boutros Boutros-Ghali about the upcoming birth of a new country — a meeting he saw as symbolic. In Washington, however, his visit was modulated so as not to upset Canadians too much. With his old friend Raymond Chrétien, Canadian Ambassador to the U.S., he agreed there should be no meeting with the president or the vice president, but only with the assistant secretary of state for political affairs. The rest of the program was similar: a private session with members of Congress and members of the Congressional study group on Canada, a speech to the Centre for Strategic and International Studies, a private lunch, a meeting with the editorial board of the Washington *Post* and a private supper at the embassy. The modest nature of the schedule did not prevent Bouchard from getting his reassuring message across. An independent Quebec would be pro–free trade, democratic and open to the world. Nor did Bouchard doubt that the Canadian economic space could be preserved. The only minor flap was provoked when Bouchard used the word *separatist* instead of *sovereignist*.

Ambassador Chrétien, the prime minister's nephew and Bouchard's friend, had made the visit as fail-safe as possible. It was easy, Bouchard says, because they worked out the schedule together. Chrétien's assistance to Bouchard was roundly criticized, especially by Reform, which saw no justification in using public funds to promote Quebec sovereignty in a foreign country. It was the prime minister himself who came to Bouchard's defence, reminding the critics that he had simply benefited from his privileges as a parliamentarian and leader of the opposition.[15]

In May, Bouchard was scheduled to visit western Canada, go to Paris and attend two meetings of Francophones outside Quebec in the same month. His message was moderate and contained no surprises. He was frank but cautious and he avoided doing or saying anything provocative. Nevertheless, the reaction was virulent. In Alberta, people he spoke with told him how disappointed they were in his proposals, emphasizing their passion for Canada. In British Columbia, he was received in the same way. No one wanted to buy his defeatist message about the future of the country. People found that he was leaving the game too quickly. British Columbia Premier Mike Harcourt said that Quebec's accession to sovereignty would be no picnic: it "may have different borders, a very bitter fight over the division, insurrections possibly with Native people and a massive exodus of people and capital."[16]

Shortly afterwards, New Brunswick Premier Frank McKenna accused Bouchard of bad faith when he learned that the sovereignist leader would come to the defence of Francophones outside Quebec during a meeting with the Francophone mayors of his province. Federal Transport Minister Doug Young, who is from New Brunswick, got carried away and called Bouchard a "Judas."

The most surprising reaction came from *Maclean's* columnist Peter C. Newman who, in a passionate plea for the survival of Canada, expressed the wish that U.S. Senator Ted Kennedy would take Bouchard for a car ride.[17] No one could mistake the innuendo. Afterwards, Newman denied that he wanted the leader of the opposition to die. He was only trying to provoke polite, apologetic Canadians into giving up their role as advocates of kindness and common sense and fighting harder for their country. Alberta Premier Ralph Klein's wish for Bouchard was no better: he hoped to see the Bloc leader treated in the same way as Métis leader Louis Riel.

The culmination of this round of passionate outbursts came with Bouchard's visit to Paris. Foreign Affairs Minister André Ouellet accused Bouchard of abusing his position as leader of the opposition. Prime Minister Chrétien maintained that the Bloc leader was fuelling economic instability. Premier Harcourt chimed in with the statement that if Quebecers "decided to separate we wouldn't be the best of friends; we'd be the worst of enemies." Saskatchewan Premier Roy Romanow, who was Jean Chrétien's ally during the 1981 constitutional negotiations, expressed approval: "I think Mike Harcourt expressed the feelings of many people in the west. Quebecers should realize, hearing these words, that it won't be an easy situation ... The idea that sovereignty could be achieved after a polite discussion around a conference table is illusory." A few days later, he added that believing in this idyllic scenario was the equivalent of believing in yogic levitation.[18]

Meanwhile, Preston Manning asked the prime minister to warn foreign countries, "and France in particular, to avoid encouraging independence directly or indirectly." He urged Chrétien to come up with a new vision for the country. Adding spice to the stew, Indian Affairs Minister Ron Irwin said that the federal government would be obliged to help Quebec aboriginals who wanted to stay in Canada.[19]

If the Bloc had been hoping to prepare a smooth transition, it had failed this time. When Bouchard finally returned home from Paris, even some sovereignists were relieved. They thought the excitement had begun a little too soon. But Bouchard was not upset: "I'm not worried by it. It was time for their real reaction to come out. They've given us a lot of show. They've given us so much show." As proof, he cites the advertisements in Quebec newspapers financed by people in western Canada telling Quebecers that westerners love them: "I always found these ads exasperating because I felt that they were window-dressing and that there was no reality behind them. Now we have it, the reality." He sees it only as a beginning and believes it is, in some cases, a strategy: "It's an attempt to make Quebecers afraid, to discourage them, to dissuade those Quebecers who might attribute a rational reaction to English Canada."

If that was the case, noted Jean-Marc Léger, the strategy's impact was opposite to its desired effect. The first rise in support for sovereignty that the pollster had recorded in two years coincided with the spirited sallies of premiers Harcourt and Romanow.

Bouchard believes that overly visceral reactions, such as Peter C. Newman's, discredit their authors in the eyes of Quebecers. He also sees them as revealing something else: "It's good because they [English Canada] are starting to take us seriously. They're lowering their guard. The mask is coming off ... I find that very healthy and very correct and it's even necessary that it happen. But we have to be careful not to provoke it." He is very touchy on this point, saying: "I have committed myself to being very, very responsible precisely to maintain a line of communication with English Canada." When people suggest that his presence in itself is provocative, he reacts: "So sovereignists have to stay at home. We can't let them think that we exist. We can't let them think that they will have a big decision to make, if we make our decision. They're the ones that have a problem, not me!"

Bouchard has always rejected the accusation that he wants to destroy a country. In his view, Canada outside Quebec is an entity, a nation that could survive by itself, and this only has to be explained to English Canadians. Gilles Rocheleau, who lives on the border between Quebec and Ontario, finds Bouchard naïve with regard to English Canada. Bouchard, he says, "is a guy who seems to forget the other facet of the pan-Canadian dynamic, because sovereignty will not be achieved easily."

Francine Lalonde has taken a number of trips to the west and met many English Canadians. She discovered that, like many other Quebecers, she had a "truncated view of Canadian power relationships." Lalonde says, "We think the power relationship is between Quebec and a kind of Ottawa-Canada that would be the other partner. It's much too shortsighted a view because you have the west, which puts a lot of pressure on Ottawa-Canada, and it's very clear that it's not just a two-player game." In her view, it is not only English Canadians who have to wake up, but Quebecers as well. She says that many people, including some of the best informed ones, "don't understand that everything we do in Quebec calls the Canadians' country into question, and they can't help becoming 'emotional.' Just because they're Anglophones, that doesn't mean they're not 'emotional.' The better I know them, the more I would be inclined to say, 'When they get emotional, they stay emotional.'"

The Bloc's Program

When the Bloc was first founded, policy was not a major priority. Lucien Bouchard notes:

> It took years before we paid attention to policy. For, I don't know, maybe two years, we didn't talk about policy. For a number of reasons. First of all, because we quite properly thought that we wouldn't be forming a government. Second, because it was very difficult to try to establish policy positions in a party that was very eclectic in its makeup. And third, because for those people in the PQ who were a bit worried about what we would eventually do with our popularity, which was just beginning to grow, not getting involved in the domain of a provincial party was a token of good faith.

But, he admits, this situation became untenable with time. The first arguments for changing it were reasons of logic: "When you advocate Quebec sovereignty, you have to be able to answer questions about what a sovereign government in Quebec City would be, how it could work." As the 1993 federal election campaign neared, the pressure increased. Voters asked questions, and the media did too. Bouchard's last remaining doubts finally gave way before the insistence of the media, and especially of Pierre Nadeau, at the time host of *L'Evénement* on the TVA television network, who put him on the hot seat and demanded to know why his party had no policies. Bouchard's pride was hurt: "It was the first time I got burned in an interview. The first time. I stickhandled as well as I could, but on my way out I said to myself: 'This is really going to become uncomfortable. We can't just complain.'"

As the party was increasingly well organized, he decided to take the plunge: the policy commission set up to advise the party on strategy and message was required to do more than draw up arguments for sovereignty and the presence of the Bloc in Ottawa. Chaired by Daniel Turp, a specialist in international law, the commission is composed of a mix of academics and other experts. "Because we had party activists, we could have a wider discussion than we could in a group of seven." Still, the policy commission and Bouchard maintained control over policy. The activists passed resolutions at a general council meeting in Quebec City in June 1993, but *Un nouveau parti pour l'étape décisive*, a reference document that would be published and sold as a book, was put together by the policy commission under Bouchard's supervision. It was essentially an explanation of what the Bloc was doing and a dissection of federalism.

Un nouveau parti stated that "there is, in Québec, a broad consensus about social and economic priorities: a significant reduction in unemployment, decentralization towards the regions and protection of social programs."[1] Advocating a combined approach to economic development, it supported continental and global trade liberalization. But the document was short on details except to explain the mission of the Bloc, its judgement of the federalist regime, and its alternative — sovereignty.

In June, the Bloc released the economic chapter of its program, but it was only during the election campaign that it issued a semblance of an overall platform. Released in stages, it was still fairly timid. In it, the Bloc proposed a $10 billion reduction in public spending per year for three years, half of which would go to cut the deficit and the rest to create jobs. Savings of $3 billion would be achieved by reducing military spending, while almost all the rest would come from eliminating fat in the operation of all government departments. There was no question of deep cuts in social programs or transfers to provinces. The Bloc's proposals included government assistance to convert military industries to civilian production and the elimination of tax shelters for the rich, especially family trusts. The party also came out in favour of free trade, financing of daycare centres and construction of a high-speed rail link in the Quebec City–Windsor corridor.

But its main theme was federal withdrawal from areas of provincial jurisdiction and an end to duplication and overlap between federal and provincial programs, again to the benefit of the provinces. The Bloc's political rhetoric, which was above all a critique of the existing system and the state of public finances, was clearly directed towards Quebec sovereignty. According to the Bloc, sovereignty would make it possible for Quebec to have the economic levers and policies it would need to solve its financial and social problems. During the election campaign, the Bloc's platform had nothing specific to offer on transportation, the environment, aboriginal affairs, immigration, or justice. On defence, it advocated a moratorium on all purchases of heavy equipment, a reevaluation of the world situation, and a one-year review of the priorities and needs of the defence department. It set as a goal a 25 per cent reduction in the military budget. But the Bloc didn't offer its own view on defence policy. In other words, *Un nouveau parti* was not the Liberal Party of Canada's Red Book, and still less the detailed platform of the Parti Québécois.

The Bloc could afford the luxury of being vague: it would never form a government. So it could be satisfied with putting forward the broad principles that would guide its actions, making it possible to have some idea of what it would do in the House of Commons, but not much more. In terms of political orientation, Bouchard set the tone during the summer and fall of 1993. "There's no way we will follow the right," he said at the start.[2]

In the middle of the campaign, he was at pains to stress the ideological differences between the Bloc and the Reform Party. "We oppose any reduction of resources for social programs," he said. [3] "Taking aim at the poor is not a way to build a society," he added later on. [4] He went as far as saying that he never was a real conservative. [5] In the end, the Bloc's positions would be defined by the caucus on a case-by-case basis.

Charting Bloc Policy

The whole ideological spectrum is represented in the Bloc, from left-leaning MPs such as Francine Lalonde and Gilles Duceppe to more conservative ones such as Nic Leblanc and Pierrette Venne. But since the 1993 election, the caucus has been mainly social-democratic in its orientation. "Sovereignty has bonded forces that otherwise, politically speaking, would not have been held together," an adviser to Bouchard acknowledges. "In practice, with what we've had to develop at the level of the Bloc Québécois, there haven't been confrontations or divergences. Probably that also has to do with the fact that the Bloc Québécois has never tried to work out a platform."

Nic Leblanc is philosophical about the way the Bloc's policy positions have evolved: "We're not here to change Canadian policies. We're here to achieve Quebec sovereignty, to make people more aware." He openly acknowledges that if Quebec becomes independent, he will undoubtedly end up in a different Quebec political party from most of his Bloc colleagues. In the meantime, he lets things be: "Personally, I yield more easily. It's temporary, I tell myself. Others do the same thing as well. People are more tolerant; they accept things more easily." He sometimes finds it funny that the party takes a position: "I laugh at it a little from time to time because I tell myself that it's temporary. We won't have time to change the world."

To arrive at a decision on a particular issue, the caucus holds debates that can last many sessions. (Twelve were held for the gun control bills.) Everyone participates, while the research office provides food for thought. Caucus chair Michel Guimond keeps the debates on track. When he thinks a consensus has emerged, he presents it to the group, which generally accepts it. But there is never a vote: this is a rule that the caucus has adopted.

In November 1993, after the election, a committee responsible for preparation of the first session wrote a guide to help the Bloc with its "strategic positioning." The committee drew up an analytical framework to help the party make its decisions in a consistent manner. No ideological objectives were set. The three points to be considered were all linked to the mission of the Bloc and the constraints of its role as official opposition. Those objectives were, in order of priority: promotion of Quebec sovereignty, defence of Quebec's immediate interests, and criticism of the government in the name of an equitable relationship between Quebec and the rest of the country.

The Bloc members also operate under a significant constraint: to avoid disunity, they have to take their fellow sovereignists in the Parti Québécois into consideration. But, Bouchard insists, the resolutions put forward by the pre-electoral general council come out of a completely independent process. Similarly, resolutions taken in caucus are arrived at independently: "We've never sat down with the Parti Québécois to talk about our platform, to talk about policy." Most of all, there is no question of submitting the Bloc's positions to a PQ imprimatur. Bouchard would not tolerate it. But his staff is in constant contact with the staffs of Jacques Parizeau and PQ House Leader Guy Chevrette. "I know what they think," Bouchard says. "I don't deliberately take aim at the PQ. When we think it could be sensitive, we tell them in advance."

Policy towards Francophones outside Quebec is the clearest example of this delicate balance. In its position, made public in Shédiac, New Brunswick in May 1994, the Bloc offered its services as the defender in Ottawa of the Francophone and Acadian communities. It also promised that a sovereign Quebec would maintain its support for French-speaking Canadians by establishing a secretariat for that purpose, among other measures. When he spoke in Shédiac, Bouchard used the occasion to apologize for Quebec's past attitudes towards the French-language minorities. "I am aware, as you are," he said, "that for three decades, the attitude of Quebec governments towards French-speaking communities in Canada has not always been marked by the degree of understanding that might have been hoped for." These remarks were not highly appreciated in the PQ, but Bouchard held his ground: "We are a federal party, and it is our mission to speak to English Canada. It's in English Canada that the Francophones outside Quebec live, and we considered it our role to put forward the elements of a vision in regard to them."

It wasn't just that the Bloc was asked to take a position on this matter. Bouchard made it a personal issue. He didn't do it to gain votes or advance a strategy. He simply wanted to build bridges with the Francophone minorities and erase the negative impression left by some sovereignists who had compared them to "corpses that are still warm." Bouchard said, "That's not what I think of them. That's not how I want Quebecers to establish a relationship with them, whether Quebec becomes sovereign or not." The Bloc is aware that this is a subject the PQ is touchy about. And so they sent the PQ a copy of the policy before it was made public. But nothing more, they emphasize. It was strictly a matter of courtesy.

While defining the Bloc's own area of concern, Bouchard has learned to stop meddling in matters that are considered provincial. In the early years of the Bloc, he was quick to express an opinion on Quebec language laws, but not any more. Policy commission chair Daniel Turp explains the decision:

> Relations among Quebecers themselves — that is, among Francophone Quebecers, Quebecers of the community of English expression and those from cultural communities — that was in the domain of Quebec's *projet de société* and so the Bloc wasn't going to take an interest in these relations. Not that it wasn't interested in them, but this was more the specific area of reflection for the Parti Québécois. So we didn't try to work out a position, a position paper on these questions.

This was why the Bloc's policy on aboriginal people, which it originally planned to release in the fall of 1994, was set aside. Earlier in the year, native affairs critic Claude Bachand and some of his colleagues had begun drawing up guidelines on native issues. Their document established six principles. They were:

- The First Nations should be recognized as distinct
- Their future should be supported by legitimate economic activities
- Natives and Canadians should consider each other as partners
- Some powers should be transferred to natives
- All citizens should receive the same level of services
- Quebec territorial integrity should be guaranteed.

Inspired by a resolution adopted in 1985 in the National Assembly, the guidelines listed some rights that any agreements concluded between natives and Canada should protect. In addition to the right to self-government, the group recognized the right of natives to protect their culture, their language and their traditions, their right to own and control lands, their right to pursue their traditional activities and participate in the management of wildlife and, finally, their right to contribute to their own economy and to benefit from it.

In the end, it was decided that this document drawn up by Bachand and his colleagues would serve as an internal guideline only. The debate on native rights was to be left to the PQ. The Bloc was not unhappy to stay out of this minefield. Native rights represent a conundrum for sovereignists. The Bloc argues that aboriginal people have the right to autonomy, but this right cannot impair the territorial integrity of an independent Quebec. In other words, the Bloc claims that Quebecers have the right to self-determination and the right to divide Canadian territory, but it denies the same right to aboriginal people. This contradictory policy also puts Daniel Turp in an odd position. Turp, who has written two theses on the right to self-determination, one at the University of Montreal and the other at Cambridge, states:

> In my academic writing, I have always upheld the idea that [the right to self-determination] includes even the right to separate, that the right to self-determination was nothing to be afraid of, and that peoples in general don't resort to the right to secede when their request for auton-

omy within a country is respected ... In Quebec, even among sovereignists, this question didn't pose too many problems until aboriginal people themselves began to invoke the right to self-determination and to demand recognition in international institutions, as they are now doing at the United Nations and elsewhere. They took and continue to take a position analogous to the one that has long been taken by Quebec sovereignists, with the support of academics such as myself — that they have the right to self-determination, the bottom line being that they have the right to separate from Canada or Quebec ... I tried to be consistent and say that logic demanded that if we uphold an idea for the Quebec people, we have to accept it for aboriginal people as well.

Turp even repeated his ideas on the right to secede before the Bélanger-Campeau Commission. In May 1994, his position again surfaced in the media, giving rise to rumours of disagreement between Bouchard and one of his leading advisers. Turp had to adjust his position in a public declaration prepared jointly with the party:

Mr. Turp wants to make it clear that he unequivocally shares the position of the leader of the Bloc Québécois, Mr. Lucien Bouchard, on the governmental autonomy of aboriginal people and Quebec's right to self-determination. Mr. Turp reiterates his position — which is also the position of the Bloc Québécois — according to which the territory of a sovereign Quebec is indivisible, in conformity with international law.

Turp maintains that he is not renouncing his academic ideas, but as soon as he decided to become part of a political process, he had to choose his priorities, and he decided "to uphold [his] main conviction, which is the conviction of a sovereignist, who wants Quebec to become a sovereign state." In his view, it is not desirable for Quebec's borders to be called into question in this context. In addition, he is convinced that a sovereign Quebec will be able to give aboriginal people the degree of autonomy they want. With an offer of a sort that they never received from Canada, they will not be inclined to demand secession. In the meantime, the Bloc would just as soon let the PQ try to disentangle itself from an issue that has been regarded as explosive ever since the Oka crisis in 1990.

With this logic, the policy commission has to carve out a very limited mandate for itself. After the 1993 election, it decided that until the prereferendum round of reflection began, it would concentrate on the Bloc's relations with English Canada and Francophones outside Quebec and on foreign affairs. But the Parti Québécois's platform is still the reference point for the Bloc. Turp says without hesitation that he feels a need to harmonize what the two parties are saying, but that doesn't mean that they always take identical positions: "There is this desire to do things together. That's clear. And it can be seen that generally, we manage to do things together without real differences on fundamentals." The Bloc is the other cog in the sovereignist machine. And so, Turp says, "We have no interest in taking positions that are seen as being in contradiction with the Parti Québécois." But Bouchard's advisers state unequivocally that the Bloc and the PQ are two separate organizations. As one says:

> We don't have the feeling here that the PQ is head office. We don't report; we don't call. What's good for the Bloc in the House of Commons, [when] we think it's the line to uphold for Quebec, we uphold it. And sometimes, what we say gives rise to a call that says, "You could have shifted a little to the left or the right." In terms of overall policy, we're tied down in some ways. But not on a day-to-day basis.

The end result of this process is surprisingly more coherent than anyone could have expected from such a heterogeneous group. Following the collapse of the NDP after the last federal election, the Bloc rapidly became the only voice of the centre-left in the House of Commons. A look at the positions it has taken on various issues is instructive.

Free Trade
On this issue, the Bloc shows its Quebec flavour. Contrary to the left in English Canada, the Bloc is in favour of the North American Free Trade Agreement (NAFTA) and trade liberalization in general. Bouchard doesn't hide the fact that he got into politics as a Conservative to defend the Meech Lake Accord and the first Free Trade Agreement (FTA) with the United States. In this respect he reflects

a consensus that has prevailed in Quebec for more than a decade, one that gave Brian Mulroney his second majority government. Quebec economic exchanges with the United States are growing faster than those with the rest of Canada, which perhaps explains interest in free trade.

During the election campaign, Bouchard made his opinion clear. "When it comes to free trade, it is a great way to implement social programs and to create resources. We will not be able to maintain the level of our social programs if we don't create economic resources. And the best way to achieve economic success is through free trade," he stated.[6] The Bloc never waivers on this subject.

The Economy and Fiscal Responsibility

The Bloc has always advocated deficit reduction but through the elimination of government waste, an end to overlapping and duplication between federal and provincial programs, severe cutbacks in defence spending and a stop to megaprojects.

Right after the 1993 federal election, the Bloc began asking the government to form a parliamentary committee that would screen all government expenses to find potential savings. Prime Minister Jean Chrétien's response was that each parliamentary committee could do part of this work when the time came to oversee the yearly budgetary estimates. The Bloc took notes and pressed a number of committees to move in this direction. The results weren't impressive.

Since then the Bloc has maintained a more traditional position, fighting against cutbacks to social programs, unemployment insurance, and provincial transfers. "Instead, Paul Martin should look for the solution in his own backyard by attacking the government's operating expenses, by revising the tax system and by attacking the underground economy that is becoming more and more apparent by the incredible amount of unpaid taxes," maintained Yvan Loubier, finance critic and MP for Saint-Hyacinthe–Bagot.

On the industrial policy front, the Bloc asked for a "genuine strategy for the conversion of defence industries to civilian production, which would both save and create new jobs in high-technology sectors." Réal Ménard, MP for Hochelaga-Maisonneuve, suggested using the money from the Defence Industry Productivity (DIP) program for this purpose. DIP encourages military production, thus inhibiting the conversion of many industries.

Concerning the GST, the Bloc tabled a minority report in June 1994 asking to have the power to collect this tax transferred to the provinces. By doing so, it said, there would only be one tax and the provinces would not be at the mercy of the federal government.

Social Programs

Close to Quebec's union movement, the Bloc has defended social democratic principles with perseverance. It is the only party to fight the Liberal's social reform proposals from a progressive point of view. Francine Lalonde, MP for Mercier, has led the fight. A former union leader, she repeated many times that the Liberals wanted to overhaul the social safety net at the expense of the less advantaged in our society. She argued that what the unemployed and people on social assistance lacked were jobs — not the will to work.

When the first parliamentary report on the subject came out on March 25, 1994, the Bloc tabled a minority report, protesting the refusal of the Standing Committee on Human Resources Development to acknowledge "the distinct character of the Quebec nation." It also denounced the majority report for not making clear that "reform of the social programs can only take place in the context of an overall policy for boosting the economy, and certainly cannot precede such a policy."

The Bloc would continue to hold this position and defend those most affected. In May 1994, it was the Bloc that forced the Liberals to extend the hearings on the budget bill and the government's drastic changes to the unemployment insurance system. The government didn't want to hear from more groups representing workers and the unemployed. The Liberals were looking bad. Then two weeks of hearings were added. Angry, the Liberals agreed to give more time to business groups established in Ottawa but refused to do the same for labour groups, some from as far away as New Brunswick. The Bloc was the only party to protest the treatment of these groups.

The Bloc disagreed with any federal attempt to get involved in job training, repeating that the money should go to the provinces which have constitutional responsibility in this area. The Bloc also vigorously maintained that the federal government should not impose national standards in health and social programs because those areas are exclusive provincial jurisdiction. Ottawa has even less justification for controlling those fields when it is reducing its financial contribution. The Bloc insisted that Ottawa should not impose conditions on its payments and should give back to the provinces the power to levy the money themselves. In this way, the provinces will not be at the mercy of policy changes coming from Ottawa.

The Bloc has also advocated more financial support for social housing, equity in the workplace for women, funding for women's groups and for battered women's shelters.

Justice

In the area of justice, the Bloc showed its Quebec distinctiveness again. When the government proposed to toughen the Young Offenders Act, the Bloc protested strenuously, maintaining that the law was perfectly adequate. It reminded the justice minister, Allan Rock, that, as shown in the polls, Quebecers believed that prevention and rehabilitation were the real key to solving youth crime and avoiding recidivism. It underlined the fact that the law was working, but to no avail. The consensus outside Quebec was to the contrary, and the law was toughened.

The Bloc distinguished itself once again when Rock tabled his hate crimes bill. The bill states that when an individual is found guilty of a crime and it is proven that his crime has been motivated by hatred, the judge should consider that as an aggravating factor when the time comes for sentencing. In the list of hate crimes targeted by the bill, the minister included those motivated by the victim's sexual orientation. The insertion of those words acted as a lightning rod for the right wing of the Liberal caucus and for the Reform party. At the end of September 1994, Reform started an all-out war against the bill. The Bloc took the opposite position, supporting the minister in including homophobia in the bill.

The Bloc went further. It pressed the justice minister to table amendments to the Human Rights Act to prohibit discrimination based on sexual orientation. On November 23, 1994, the MP for Hochelaga-Maisonneuve, Réal Ménard, also tabled a bill to give equal rights to same-sex couples.

However, the Bloc showed it was a party like the others when it bent, in some ways, to put pressure on gun-control legislation. For more than one year, the Bloc supported a tightening of gun-control legislation. In May 1994, Pierrette Venne, the justice critic, asked for a total ban on all handguns, mandatory registration of all firearms and a mandatory permit for purchasing ammunition. A hunter herself, Venne was not new to this issue. She had started asking for more restrictions when she was in the Conservative caucus.

Now, with the backing of the Bloc caucus, she defended registration, sanctions for non-compliers, tougher sentences for crimes committed with a firearm, and so on. Allan Rock, confronted with opposition in the Liberal caucus and the opposition of the Reform party, came to count on the support of the Bloc. But on May 17, 1995, Pierrette Venne, obviously upset, held a press conference to announce that her party would present amendments. The Bloc was not rejecting the bill altogether. Registration was not in question, although the Bloc suggested accelerating the registration process. But the sanctions proposed for not registering a rifle or for committing a crime with a gun were lighter.

"As soon as you start talking about firearms, males get worked up and overexcited, unfortunately, but that's the way it is. And as you know, in the Bloc, women are not in the majority, so we certainly had a lot of pressure from the male members of the caucus," she told the press. She was then referring mainly to the rural MPs of the Bloc who had heard, like their colleagues in other parties, the complaints of hunters and gun owners.

Labour

On labour issues, the Bloc again showed its sympathy for unions and workers. In March 1995, just before the national rail strike, the Bloc tabled an anti-scab bill. Inspired by the legislation adopted in Quebec in 1977, Bernard Saint-Laurent, MP for Manicouagan, proposed forbiding the hiring of strikebreakers by employers under federal jurisdiction, crown corporations or the Canadian public service. To compensate, he recommended that the legislation ensure the maintenance of essential services during a strike or lock-out within the public service or a crown corporation. For the Bloc, that legislation would force both parties to negotiate. "An anti-scab law represents respect and dignity for the workers," explained Saint-Laurent.

But the Bloc really distinguished itself at the end of March 1995, during the national rail strike. The strike began on a Saturday night. The Liberal government immediately announced it would present back-to-work legislation the following Monday. The Bloc refused to give its consent before seeing the bill. When the Bloc MPs saw it, they declared it unacceptable for workers, because it imposed arbitration after one month of mediation. The Bloc asked for a sixty-day period of mediation followed by a new debate in Parliament before forcing any settlement. The government refused. All the Bloc could do was to force the government to follow all the steps of parliamentary procedure. Thus, it succeeded in delaying the final adoption of the bill for one week.

The government, the business community and the press, especially in English Canada, accused the Bloc of only looking for a way to disrupt the Canadian economy. Bouchard was furious that his party was being criticized for only doing its job and for asking that the parliamentary rules be respected in the name of the workers. After the first round, even the NDP, the traditional pro-labour party, abandoned the Bloc, and the Bloc found itself alone in its opposition to the legislation. "There is a right-wing current in this House where it is not politically correct to defend the right to strike. There will be at least one party to defend the workers and it will be us," Bouchard told the press after four days of fighting.

Health

The main health issue taken up by the Bloc has been the tainted blood scandal. This scandal occurred during the early eighties when hundreds of hemophiliacs and surgery patients were contaminated by HIV through blood products and blood transfusions. Since January 1994, a week has seldom passed without the Bloc raising the issue, asking the government to do more to reassure Canadians on the blood supply system, tighten the quality controls, improve the coordination between responsible agencies, and so on. In the spring of 1995, the Bloc went so far as to ask for criminal charges against those responsible for the delay in the HIV testing of the blood and the distribution of safe products to hemophiliacs.

The Bloc also pressed the health minister, Diane Marleau, without success for an answer to the report on New Reproductive Technologies tabled in November 1993. The Bloc believes that Ottawa should act more expeditiously to prohibit embryonic research aimed at cloning, the creation of animal-human hybrids and the transfer of human embryos to other species. It should also prohibit sex preselection of newborns, regulate or prohibit the market in surrogate mothers and completely prohibit certain techniques or practices like the sale of ova, sperm, embryos, fetuses or fetal tissue for commercial purposes.

Culture

In the cultural arena, the Bloc has concentrated mainly on attacking the credibility of the heritage minister, Michel Dupuy, after he wrote to the CRTC to support an application for a radio licence by one resident of his riding. The Bloc also attacked him for a trip to Los Angeles and for his handling of the issue of direct-to-home satellite TV.

The cuts to cultural institutions, especially the CBC, were the other main concern. The Bloc maintains that the French CBC should not be affected as much as the English service. According to the Bloc, the French network, which is successful, should not pay for the difficulties of English language television. When the new heads of the CBC were named at the end of March 1995, the heritage critic, Suzanne Tremblay, MP for Rimouski-Témiscouata, again voiced her concern and underlined that the new president of the CBC, Perrin Beatty, was unable to name one French TV show during his press conference.

The Bloc also pushed for amendments to the Copyright Act to give better protection to artists. In the spring of 1994, the Bloc tried to stir a debate on the management of the Canadian Museum of Nature and the slow diminution of its scientific capability. The Bloc was echoing the concerns of many universities and a number of scientists, but the issue didn't fly except in the Ottawa region, where the museum is located.

Ethics

On March 11, 1994, Louis Plamondon tabled a motion in the House calling for the introduction of public financing of political parties in Canada, a system similar to the one in place in Quebec since 1977. It proposed to limit to individuals the right to contribute to the financing of any federal party and to restrict the contributions to $5,000 per year, rules the Bloc had imposed on itself since the beginning. The reason for the proposals, stated the Bloc, was to free political parties of the influence of big corporations. The motion was defeated on September 27, 1994.

On the issue of lobbyist registration, the Bloc takes the high road. It wants a stricter control so lobbyists would have to reveal their honoraria and which ministers and public servants they have contacted. The Bloc would also eliminate the tax deduction for the hiring of lobbyists. Finally, the Bloc would like the ethics counsellor to answer to Parliament and not to the prime minister.

Foreign Affairs

In the fall 1993 issue of *Canadian Foreign Policy*, Michel Fortmann and Gordon Mace wrote that it was difficult to anticipate what the Bloc would say on international affairs. Their only solution, they said, was to refer to the Bloc's closest ally, the PQ. Since then, Bouchard has taken the comment to heart. As foreign affairs critic, he clarified the position of the party. He believes Canada's traditional foreign policy is a great heritage that deserves to be pursued.

As a supporter of multilateralism, Bouchard advocated a reform of UN institutions, an enlargement of the Security Council, the reform of NATO, and a reevaluation of NORAD before renewing the agreement in 1996. The Bloc favoured the Gérin-Lajoie doctrine, a Quebec position that advocates that the provinces, especially Quebec, be able to sign treaties and participate in international organizations in areas that pertain to their exclusive powers.

The Bloc also advocates maintaining a link between trade and human rights and advocates that Canada take a more proactive stance in defending rights and freedoms. Bouchard denounced in this regard the timidity of Prime Minister Jean Chrétien during his first trip to Asia, especially when he visited China and Indonesia.

Bouchard is a strong defender of foreign aid, recommending that it should mainly serve long-term development, be more concentrated and distributed with a special focus on Africa. "We should avoid demagogy when we talk of foreign aid. It is not wasted money. Canada has obligations toward the poorest and it cannot let the gap widen between rich and poor," repeated Bouchard.[7]

In its minority report on defence policy review, the Bloc reiterated its support for peacekeeping but suggested adjustments. "Canada's resources are too limited for it to get involved in every theatre of conflict," stated the Bloc members on the review committee, Jean-Marc Jacob, MP for Charlesbourg, and Jean Leroux, MP for Shefford. They proposed to establish priorities for involvement based on criteria to be defined, to set a ceiling on the human resources committed to peacekeeping and to send only specially trained military personnel. They recommended that Canada require UN reform of its chain of command. At the same time, they suggested the creation of a permanent international contingent available to the UN for peacekeeping. Bloc members strongly support the expansion of the Nuclear Non-proliferation Treaty.

On the issue of defence in general, the Bloc advocates a rationalization of expenditures and personnel, especially a reduction in the number of officers.

Quebec Independence

The issue that is naturally of most interest to the public is the Bloc's position on the process of accession to sovereignty. Where does the Bloc stand on the issue, especially in relation to the PQ?

In the spring of 1993, the PQ and the Bloc released manifestoes to explain their projects. In *Quebec in a New World*, Jacques Parizeau explained that a sovereign Québec will offer Canada an agreement on association to maintain the economic union between the two states. This economic union, Parizeau stated, will include a monetary union, a customs union and free circulation of goods, services, capital and individuals. He underlined that some elements — the use of the dollar, for example — can be maintained without Canada's consent.

To oversee and manage this association, some institutions would be necessary, indicated Parizeau. He envisaged three of them. First, a ministerial council where ministers or delegates from each state would make decisions on matters provided for in the treaty between Canada and Quebec. Second, a secretariat would be responsible for the implementation of the treaty under the direction of the council. Finally, a tribunal would serve as a dispute-settlement mechanism. Parizeau elaborated that he doesn't exclude a discussion on Quebec's participation in the Bank of Canada or the establishment of bilateral commissions on specific aspects of the treaty.

In May 1993 in *Un nouveau parti pour l'étape décisive*, the Bloc went further than the PQ in making direct references to the European model. Contrary to the PQ leader, who didn't take for granted that Canada would agree on everything, the Bloc document was more affirmative.[8] "The free movement of people, capital, goods and services already exists inside the Canadian economic space. The harmonization is done. The single currency exists. In other words, the economic integration of a sovereign Quebec and Canada would be, at the start, as deep as what would eventually follow the Maastricht Treaty for the European Community," stated the document, which was written under Bouchard's supervision.[9] "The Quebec-Canada treaty will not necessarily have the same architecture as the Treaty of Rome of 1957. But there will be a treaty."[10]

Like the PQ, the Bloc wants to maintain monetary and customs unions. Bouchard requires that Quebec have a say in the monetary policy of the Bank of Canada. To implement the treaty, he suggests common institutions but without being very precise. Using the same terms as the European Union, he simply says: "We can imagine common institutions (council, commission and tribunal) to manage the Canada-Quebec economic space and specific mechanisms to harmonize policies in areas like defense and security, protection of minority rights, environment, native relations ... And we should not exclude the creation of a Common Parliamentary Conference that could be a discussion forum on community issues."

Bouchard, however, is convinced that Canada does not want to talk about the constitution. So why does he think Canada would agree to negotiate all this with an independent Quebec? Out of common sense and because it won't have a choice, he maintains. "I know very well that there will be no proposal coming from English Canada. [But] as long as there is no referendum on sovereignty, in which Quebecers say yes, English Canadians won't budge." But once the dust has settled, he told the *Financial Post* in December 1993, he is "convinced it will be English Canada that will seek [an association] if for no other reason than to pay the debt."[11] And the purpose of his pilgrimage across Canada was to get beyond the political shadow-boxing.

If English Canada remains obstinate, Bouchard reminds his audiences, Quebec can continue to use the Canadian dollar without asking permission. He forgets to mention that in this situation, Quebec would be subject to the monetary policy of another country without its economic interests being taken into consideration. "It will be in English Canada's interest to negotiate and talk with a Quebec that wants to become sovereign, if only to maintain the economic space and exports to Quebec — which represent 100,000 jobs in Ontario alone! To avoid the irrational reactions that they might be tempted to have, we have to prepare them to talk with Quebec," he told *L'Actualité*. "We have always said that English Canadians will sit down at the table and talk with us because it will be in their interest ... If we prepare Canadians, they will think it over. We know that the Ontario establishment wants to negotiate. They're not crazy."[12]

Bouchard believes that the Bloc's work before a referendum on sovereignty can make it possible for English Canada to let off steam, so that when the day comes, heads will be cooler. But it is not clear with whom Bouchard wants to negotiate. Commentators are quick to criticize him for his monolithic view of the country. "The sticking point here is Mr. Bouchard's implication that these negotiations have to be between Quebec and English Canada as two apparently separate entities," wrote Robert Sheppard in the Toronto *Globe and Mail* just two days after Bouchard resigned from the cabinet, "as if Parliament and the various provincial legislatures might not have their own individual interests to bring to the table — not to mention natives and other important interest groups."[13] This criticism has persisted until today.

Bouchard has always maintained that Canadians outside Quebec have a clear and uniform idea of the country they want — a strong central government with equal provinces subordinate to it. He points out that Quebec's traditional demands run counter to this model and cannot be accommodated within it, summing up the situation with an aphorism: "There is a country missing in this country." He even concludes that Quebec sovereignty represents an opportunity for the rest of Canada, because it could set up the system it wants.

For the Bloc, then, the main thrust of its interventions in the House remains Quebec's interests or point of view. Most of the time, the Bloc is engaged in denouncing any project seen as centralist, condemning federal action in areas of provincial jurisdiction or taking a position in conformity with Quebec public opinion. Occasionally, the Bloc strays toward more folkloric gestures like the tabling of a bill to declare Louis Riel innocent, the tabling of motions recognizing the contribution of the rebels of 1837 in Upper and Lower Canada to the establishment of democratic institutions in Canada or the request for compensation for the persons arrested without cause during the 1970 October Crisis. But the consensus in general is that the Bloc has carved a special place for itself in the Canadian political spectrum and it is one that expresses the distinctiveness of Quebec's social democrats.

Solidarity Among Sovereignists?

In June 1994, after playing the lead for six months, Bouchard had to step aside. It was his turn to play a supporting role. With the help of the PQ, he had fulfilled his part of the bargain in carrying out the sovereignist initiative. Now it was his turn to help the PQ depose the Liberals in the provincial election campaign.

As in the 1993 federal election campaign, the special advisers to Bouchard and Parizeau, Pierre-Paul Roy and Jean Royer, worked closely to define the role Bouchard and the Bloc would play in the 1994 provincial campaign. They began their discussions on strategic coordination in the spring. Meanwhile, the leaders' chiefs of staff, Gilbert Charland of the Bloc and Hubert Thibault of the PQ, discussed policy and the message that would be conveyed. François Leblanc of the Bloc and Pierre Boileau of the PQ cooperated on the organizational side. The PQ was clearly in the driver's seat and the Bloc, with its limited means, was there to provide what assistance it could. Its main contribution was expected to be the availability of its leader, who would put his popularity to work for the PQ's benefit in the regions.

The harmonious collaboration of the two parties' general staffs was a repetition of 1993. On the ground, the situation was also similar to what had gone on one year earlier. In Montreal, for example, PQ candidates Louise Harel and Jean Campeau met with Bloc MPs Gilles Duceppe and Michel Daviault each week to analyze events and discuss the campaign. In other areas, however, there was friction. "The PQ ran its campaign and wasn't concerned at all about the Bloc MPs," says one Bloc member. "There were ridings where the MP wasn't invited to a single meeting. It was their game, their election."

Nevertheless, the campaign went well. As Bouchard trudged through small-town Quebec, the metropolitan press quickly lost interest in his tour. Bouchard maintains he was relieved when he got rid of his media escort. He felt that the press was only in search of contradictions between his position and Parizeau's. He had a taste of this medicine at the start of his campaign. As soon as he got back on August 3, 1994 from his holiday in California, he was asked about the PQ promise to have the National Assembly adopt a solemn declaration stating Quebec's wish to become sovereign. Bouchard told the press that "sovereignty will have to be decided by a referendum." Bouchard believed the election and the referendum should be two distinct exercises. "First of all, the election of a new government in Quebec and then a referendum. People know very well in Quebec that there will be two different decisions taken through different processes," he said.[1]

The next day, he repeated his stance. "The National Assembly cannot replace the population," he maintained, drawing attention to a point of view that differed from Parizeau's.[2] On August 7, in Joliette, the two leaders agreed on the line to take. "At first, a government, and then sovereignty" was their new motto, in effect endorsing Bouchard's position.

Once this incident was behind him, Bouchard tried to discourage the reporters who were following him. "Two people with a microphone in front of them during an election campaign cannot work. There are too many opportunities to differ on very small points," he said. As for the Bloc MPs and staff, they were relegated to the sidelines during the campaign. From their vantage point there, they didn't always like what they saw. Bloc staff members were aware of weaknesses in the PQ's campaign, especially in the areas of advertising and the failure of its organization to work full-tilt to the end.

Denis Monière, who analyzed the campaign, was critical of the PQ advertising strategy. He observed a disparity between the two main parties. The Liberals produced thirty-nine different commercials, half of them attacking sovereignty and bought three times as much air time as the PQ. The PQ referred to sovereignty only once in its commercials, which were repetitious and unconnected with the campaign in the field, Monière found. Pollster Jean-Marc Léger notes that the PQ lost ground late in the campaign, especially in the last four days. At the end, Premier Daniel Johnson was campaigning energetically and he seemed to be the only one running. He effectively turned the campaign into a referendum, without any response from the PQ. "Sovereignty dragged the PQ down in this campaign," Léger suggests. "In the second to last week of the campaign, sovereignty was at 40 per cent and the PQ was at 49 per cent." The PQ ended up splitting the difference between those two figures with just under 45 per cent of the vote.

On election night, September 12, 1994, the PQ victory had a slightly bitter taste. The PQ formed a majority government, but with only 13,744 votes more than the Liberals. The PQ received 44.75 per cent of the vote compared to the Liberals' 44.4 per cent. There were no smiles on the faces of the winners, especially Bouchard's. He and his team did not join the PQ victory party, preferring instead to celebrate in Bouchard's suite at the Château Frontenac. Bouchard knew the results meant a steeper road to winning the referendum and he was not thrilled by this prospect. In the days that followed, Bouchard did not hide his disappointment. "I had hoped [support] would be somewhere around 48 per cent and maybe more," he told a CTV interviewer. He concluded that it had been a mistake not to reply to Daniel Johnson's attacks on sovereignty, a peculiar criticism from a man who insisted that the campaign be about the election of a new government and that the sovereignty issue be resolved later on, during a referendum.[3]

This hair's-breadth victory did not augur well for the PQ. Bouchard decided to send a clear message to the sovereignists and to the PQ in particular. The message was that losing the referendum could not be an option and should be avoided at any price, even if it meant a delay. Surrounded by his staff, he met the press in the lobby of the House of Commons for the first daily scrum of the session. "What's important is to win," he said. "To lose the referendum doesn't make sense."[4] During the following days, he repeated his message in several interviews. He was casting doubt on Parizeau's 1995 referendum schedule at a time when the premier was in seclusion to form his cabinet and not accessible to the media.

Bouchard's position was not new, but it was the first time he had expressed it in public. In March 1994, his advisers came to the conclusion that a victory with less than 45 per cent of the vote would be a source of problems. "The electoral momentum has to be impressive," was one adviser's analysis at the time. "In other words, 43 or 44 per cent is not what you would consider enough to put us ahead in the referendum."

Bouchard took advantage of exchanges with the press to convey a message to his political allies. "When I answer [a question from the press], I say what I think and I try to do it correctly and in a manner that won't rock the boat. At the same time, it permits me to establish the parameters of some positions we believe we will hold in the future." He adds that he doesn't need the media to communicate with Jacques Parizeau, but he admits that on the day that he talked about the necessity of winning a referendum, he was deliberately sending a message to the new team in power at Quebec.

"I felt it necessary to mention that a referendum had to be a winning one and to remind people of the harmful consequences of a defeat." Bouchard explains he was pressed to act that way because Jacques Parizeau had made a statement, at the end of the campaign, minimizing the consequences of a No vote. "This and the election results made me think that people had to be reminded that losing a referendum was not a small affair, that they should instead get organized to win it," he explains.

But Bouchard's uncompromising statements on the referendum timetable and his heavy-handed approach created a tense atmosphere. To some extent, the Bloc leader was settling old scores. He was frustrated at being kept in the dark about what was going on in Quebec City in the days following the election. Eleven days passed before Bouchard was able to meet with Parizeau. In the end, the wrinkles caused by Bouchard's comments were ironed out expeditiously, and cooperation was reestablished. Both parties had no choice. The timetable was too tight to waste time bickering.

A Mouthpiece for Sovereignty

In Parliament, the PQ election victory cast a new light on the Bloc's ways of doing things. As early as June 1994, Bouchard had predicted that his party would turn itself into a "conveyer belt" for the Quebec government in the House of Commons. He was overjoyed at this prospect. He saw the Bloc as finally fulfilling its true role, the one for which it had been conceived "from the beginning." He said, "This is what the Bloc will really be. Live and instantaneously, transmission of Quebec's political and governmental will to the House of Commons." It didn't much matter to Bouchard that the Bloc would be in an awkward position with regard to its role as the official opposition: "We've always been in an awkward position. It will be a little more awkward." He was relieved to be able to devote himself to his reason for being in politics for the past four years — sovereignty.

Bloc MPs acknowledged that this shift of focus would have an impact. "Not only will we no longer be the main spokespeople for Quebec in English Canada," Francine Lalonde said anxiously at the time, "but we will also appear to be the enemies within." Nor would the Bloc MPs be as visible now that they had to compete with the people who were really running things: the members of the PQ cabinet. "It's not the Bloc's [story] any more. Now the Bloc has to play a supporting role. As long as the Parti Québécois was in opposition, the Bloc had a lot of presence and prestige," notes Monière.

Jean Lapierre, who has remained close to Bouchard, believes that this situation is extremely frustrating. He compares Parizeau to someone driving a motorcycle, while Bouchard is riding in the sidecar. The Bloc shadow cabinet could be highly constrained because they have to take into account what's being said in Quebec City. The relationship is no longer one of equal to equal, MP to MNA, but rather one of MP to minister. "They are completely dependent on what happens in Quebec City," Lapierre says, and with a sigh he exclaims, "They're just a cog in the machine! The head office has been moved to the bunker—it's only natural. The rest is just nuance, subtleties for the benefit of reporters. They're almost as closely bound by cabinet solidarity as the members of the cabinet themselves."

During the first few months following the provincial election, Bouchard's frustration and that of the Bloc members was not apparent. On the contrary, organizational relations between the PQ and the Bloc reached an unprecedented level of intimacy. The two leaders worked out the main elements of the referendum strategy together. The idea of commissions to consult Quebecers had been in the air since the summer. This was not surprising. From 1990 on, Bouchard and Parizeau had always wanted to see the referendum preceded by a consultation, in an effort to create momentum and a consensus among Quebecers. The only new twist was the formula. On December 6, 1994, Parizeau announced that fifteen regional commissions (eventually sixteen) and two special commissions would take the people's pulse on a bill to make Quebec a sovereign state.

Originally, Parizeau had planned for a different process. At first, the PQ stated that a Parti Québécois government would "submit to the National Assembly for adoption a solemn declaration stating Quebec's wish to accede to full sovereignty" after an election. Then, it would hold "discussions" with the federal government, following which he would "establish the timetable and modalities for transferring powers and determine the rules for dividing Canada's assets and debts." The National Assembly was to have adopted legislation instituting a constitutional commission. A referendum on sovereignty should be held as soon as possible. Finally, the program had stated that the Quebec government would propose "mutually advantageous forms of economic association to the federal government. These proposals will include the institution of joint bodies, established through treaties, to manage the economic relationship between Canada and Quebec."

The election results, the polls and the pressure of his allies forced Parizeau to modify his course.With the help of his inner circle and with the support of Bouchard, he put forward a seventeen-point draft bill which would be debated in commissions, voted on by the National Assembly but could not be proclaimed before being endorsed by the population in a referendum. Quebec voters would then be asked: "Are you in favour of the act passed by the National Assembly declaring the sovereignty of Quebec? Yes or No." The plan was that Quebec would become a sovereign country within one year of a Yes vote. After that, negotiations with the rest of Canada on an economic partnership would start.

The draft bill defined sovereignty as the capacity for Quebec to have exclusive jurisdiction over its laws, levy all taxes, and have the exclusive right to participate in international treaties and organizations. According to the draft legislation, Quebec would use the Canadian dollar, retain its territory, permit dual citizenship, initiate talks on Quebec's share of the federal debt and assets, maintain pension payments to the elderly, and constitutionally entrench the Anglophone minority's historic rights and the natives' right to self-government within Quebec's borders.

In preparing for the referendum, lines blurred as the organizations of the two parties moved towards fusion. The Bloc was getting closer to the PQ machine. At the end of November 1994, some Bloc members wondered what impact this fact would have on the Bloc's ability to be a rallying force. They tried to raise this question at the party's general council, but without success. The subject was debated in a few regional workshops, when journalists were not in sight, but that was all. Nobody was interested in talking publicly about it, especially not the party leadership. Bouchard himself spoke glowingly of the "osmosis" between the two organizations.

On December 9, 1994, the two parties announced the creation of a joint referendum committee to coordinate the early stages of the campaign. The PQ mobilized its major figures. A week later, the committee met and announced that the organizations of the two parties would merge in preparation for the referendum. Coming out of the meeting, Quebec Deputy Premier Bernard Landry said that its goal had been "to join forces as if, in operational terms, there was now only one party." [5] The PQ and the Bloc consulted on the makeup of the regional commissions and even adopted a joint strategy document in mid-January 1995.

Bouchard had no illusions about who had the power to press the right buttons. Parizeau, he said, "will be chair of the Yes committee. He will hold all the reins in his hands, much more than before the Charlottetown referendum. He will decide how roles will be distributed. He is the one who will decide, in accordance with what he thinks will be most favourable to the success of the referendum." But Bouchard would also have a central role to play. As the most popular politician in Quebec and the driving force behind the Bloc, his participation would be crucial.

Then, on November 29, Bouchard was struck by necrotizing myositis, popularly known as "flesh-eating disease." He was admitted to Montreal's Saint-Luc Hospital, and on November 30 his left leg was amputated at mid-thigh. As rumours began to fly and many expected the worst, there was widespread speculation about what effect his illness would have on the sovereignist camp, especially since his doctors were talking about a rehabilitation period that could last three or four months. But to everyone's amazement, Bouchard quickly resumed control. Less than a week after being admitted to hospital, he was distributing instructions and responsibilities to his MPs and put his chief of staff, Gilbert Charland, in charge. In early January, he was sufficiently alert to undertake a reshuffling of the party's senior staff and to write a letter to be used in the prereferendum fundraising campaign. But his first public appearance, which everyone was anxiously awaiting, was still weeks away.

During his absence, the commissions were put together and Parizeau surprised everyone by appointing two former Conservative ministers, Marcel Masse and Monique Vézina, to head the Montreal commission and the commission for the elderly respectively. The mayor of Quebec City, Jean-Paul L'Allier, agreed to chair his city's commission. Things seemed to go well. A SOM poll published on December 9 showed that if the population didn't support sovereignty (43 per cent supported the Yes side; 57 per cent No), it agreed with the process put in place by the PQ government. Sixty-eight per cent of the 1,022 Quebecers reached by the pollster believed that federalists should participate in this process. [6]

Jacques Parizeau also succeeded in swaying another player, the young leader of the Parti de l'Action Démocratique du Québec

(ADQ), Mario Dumont. Dumont was an important catch for Parizeau. The young man might be the ADQ's only MNA, but he still represented 6.5 per cent of the population, a figure that could make a difference between a defeat or a victory in the referendum.

Going home for Christmas, Parizeau looked like he had the momentum on his side. But in February, when the commissions began their public hearings, things didn't unfold as predicted. A cacophony of interests and concerns was expressed. About 55,000 people participated, and they asked for everything from the legalization of video gambling to improved history classes. Nevertheless, some broad themes emerged from the briefs and in the public forums: a new social contract, the decentralization of powers in favour of the regions and the preservation of the Canadian economic space.

At the same time, two federal byelections were going on in Quebec, one in the Liberal stronghold of Saint-Henri–Westmount and the other in the riding of Brome-Missisquoi, in the Eastern Townships. The latter riding had been represented by the Bloc MP Gaston Péloquin who died suddenly in a car accident on September 1, 1994. The campaign to replace him rapidly took on a referendum flavour and polarized the voters. In the end, on February 13, the Bloc candidate, Jean-François Bertrand, a former PQ cabinet minister and the son of late premier Jean-Jacques Bertrand, did better than Péloquin in 1993, but it was not enough. Liberal Denis Paradis concentrated the rest of the vote and won.

Just after that, the CBC released a poll showing that a referendum held in February would have the same result as the 1980 referendum. That is, 60 per cent of the population would vote No and 40 per cent Yes. It left the impression that sovereignists were driving full speed into a wall.

It was at this time that Bouchard put an end to his convalescence. He announced it at the beginning of the month in the form of a letter to the U.S. authorities asking for a meeting with President Bill Clinton during his visit to Ottawa on February 23 and 24.

Bouchard's comeback had been anxiously anticipated. He knew it and, deliberately or not, he managed to make it unusual. The conventional press conference was not planned as the start of his journey but as the culmination of four days of media exposure. This media management sparked a wave of criticism from a number of news outlets, but in the end, what Bouchard said—and he said a lot—grabbed the spotlight.

Recalling his fight for his life, he said he was moved by the support he had received from all across the country. It didn't change his political beliefs, but it made him wonder about a country where people always had civilized relations but were unable to find collective solutions to old fights.

In all his public appearances, politics wasn't far in the background. It didn't take long for him to wonder aloud about the proposed referendum question. His musing added to a debate that began during the regional commissions and was echoed on February 17 by Jacques Parizeau. "There's definitely a hitch with the question," said the premier.[7] Bouchard's statement reinforced the jockeying. He wanted a "frank, direct and clear question" but not the one in the draft bill. "I would change it, I would work on it," he told the *Globe's* Suzanne Delacourt. "I never committed myself to a specific drafting of the question," he added.[8] But at his press conference, he admitted that, at first, he had no problem with it, that it was the polls that changed his mind. He still wanted a question on sovereignty but he wanted it also to reflect the necessary compromises that would guarantee a victory. "Something which would make Quebec move ahead in the direction of sovereignty," he told *Canada AM*.[9]

He went further, talking about strategy, and once again questioning the referendum timetable. He even considered the possibility of not holding a referendum. "I don't think that Mr Parizeau could delay the referendum *sine die* after 1995. He's leading a government, he has to make decision and it's like the sword of Damocles. He will have to call a referendum or decide not to call one. It's a terrible decision he will have to made. Personally, I think that no one should ever deliberately expose Quebec to a No. So he will have to use his judgement," he said on *The Fifth Estate*.[10]

Bouchard expressed the opinion that the commissions were useful, but he had doubts on the steps that were to follow. "I feel that the full strength of Quebecers, all their solidarity, is not made use of. It lies fallow and I don't like that," he told *Le Soleil*.[11] He took advantage of his interviews to advise Parizeau to "take a decision to launch the referendum according to Quebec's interest," which means to be sure it had a reasonable chance to win. From one interview to another, Bouchard repeated his warnings. Clearly, if he came back from his illness faster than expected, it was not only because he was bored. He seemed genuinely to feel the situation was urgent; that somebody should ring the bell about the danger of a speedy referendum and the risks inherent in failure.

A few statements raised eyebrows and cast doubts on the sincerity of his motives. It started in a *Le Point* interview when he was questioned on the message he wrote when he was struggling for his life. "Que l'on continue, merci!" (Carry on. Thank you!) What did it mean, asked Jean-François Lépine.

> I remember that my surgeon, who was supposed to hold a press conference the same day or the day after, asked me if I had a message. At this point, I was sure of nothing, nothing concerning my own future, and I thought that it would be stupid to stop. So I wrote, in almost illegible characters ... those words, "Carry on," without thinking about the immediate political repercussions. But I had in my mind the idea that we should not stop there, that we had to continue, that Quebec's future was more than a poll, more than a discouraging poll, more than a moment's hesitation ... that it had to be more than one individual's fate.

"So it really was a political message?" asked Lépine.

"Oh yes, it was political, I modestly confess, it was political," replied the Bloc's leader.[12]

For the parliamentary press corps, that statement came as a surprise. In December, Bouchard's staff had insisted that the message was intended only for his physicians and that anyone who thought otherwise was being cynical. The new meaning given to the message by Bouchard in February added to feelings of distaste about the management of his return to public life and left journalists wondering about his intentions. This time, it was the Bloc leader who was being cynical and sounding more or less like any other politician.

The reaction of the press must have reached Bouchard because in the following TV interviews, he changed his stand. On *The Fifth Estate,* he even maintained the contrary. "I never knew that they would be published and have a political character," he said of his words. But he added in the same breath that there was more to it than a simple message to his doctors. "It was also related to the fact that whatever happens to individuals, it doesn't change the flow of things for society," he continued.[13]

Bouchard left another question mark, this time about his political ambitions, a subject of numerous rumours over the years, which he had never succeeded in completely dissipating. He told *Le Soleil* that he missed the political arena but his illness had taught him to fight "for the real things ... There are things going on and there are things I would like to say. I've been in politics for five years and I never did anything really important. I only built base camps for others who wanted to climb Everest. I spent five years doing that, but the summit is still there and, at a certain point, you have to go for the summit!" He added that he was "nobody's conscript ... I don't take the decisions, but each of us remains master of their personal reactions," he continued.[14]

Those metaphors caught the public imagination. At his press conference, journalists wanted to know what Everest was for him. A number of them believed he was thinking of Parizeau's job. He explained that he was talking about sovereignty, the need for Quebecers to reach the summit. But then, he added, "It is possible that unconsciously I was thinking of myself because I thought a lot about my political career, about my presence in politics, whether I should continue."[15] A month later, in his office, still struggling to sit comfortably after his convalescence, he once again maintained that he no longer wanted to stay on the sidelines, always thinking of returning to his law practice.

Bouchard came back with a specific idea in his mind. In February, during his media reentry, he threw out some clues, here and there, about what he called a *virage* or sharp turn that he planned to impose on the sovereignist boat. To *Le Soleil,* he hinted that he had begun to work on "a major speech on sovereignty." He wanted the movement to renew its thinking and get the debate on a new track. Asked at his press conference if he was still advocating the European model when he talked about a "question that would move Quebec towards sovereignty," he answered that nothing "positive, interesting and creative" should be excluded. He added later on that "maybe some other people need more explanation on what sovereignty will be, what it will mean in terms of an economic link with the rest of Canada, things like that. We will see."

During the visit of U.S. President Bill Clinton, Bouchard continued to make news. As leader of the official opposition, he got his private meeting with the president, a first in Canadian history. Never before had a sovereignist leader met with a U.S. head of state. Nothing spectacular emerged from the meeting, but the mere fact that it had taken place at all drew attention.

Bouchard's orchestrated comeback showed that he wanted a share of the centre stage. He didn't see himself as second fiddle. "After having conquered my political freedom, I want to keep it," he told the press.[16] He didn't dispute the fact that Parizeau had the power as premier, but Bouchard's manner demonstrated his acute awareness of his own strength, his higher popular support.

The Slippery Slope

Bouchard's statements after his illness added to the state of confusion and to the tensions beginning to plague the sovereignist camp. It was at this moment that Parizeau decided to go to Mexico for a short holiday. During his absence, nothing seemed under control. Bouchard, once again, fed the press. The referendum question, he said on February 28, should be on sovereignty but should also mention an economic union with the rest of Canada. In Quebec City, the reaction was cool. Senior ministers underlined that the regional commissions were still going on and that the inclusion of economic association in the draft bill was being considered. Mario Dumont and certain other sovereignists suggested asking for a negotiating mandate, as had been done in 1980. Some PQ MNAs were publicly casting doubt on the question and the date of the referendum.

When Parizeau came back on March 8, his reaction was swift. He first restated that the referendum should be held in 1995. Then he rejected the idea of a negotiating mandate, but kept his mind open to Bouchard's proposal. "I want to see all the questions that have been suggested and discuss it with the Bloc Québécois people, as long as it doesn't denature the draft bill," he said, adding that he wanted to wait for the regional commissions' reports expected the following week.[17]

Boycotted by the federalists, most commissions produced pro-sovereignty reports but not without nuances and some clear demands. People wanted to know how sovereignty could change things for the better. Everywhere people longed for a new social contract, wanted more information on how an economic association with Canada would work and insisted on a clear question on sovereignty. The majority rejected the constitutional status quo and endorsed the idea that a defeat should be avoided, even if it meant adopting a more moderate pace to the referendum Bouchard took note as he was privately working with his team on a new sovereignist plan. He was able to count on a new adviser, Jean-François Bertrand, his defeated candidate in Brome-Missisquoi, who joined his team on March 3. A former supporter of René Lévesque's stand on sovereignty-association, Bertrand stayed on when Pierre Marc Johnson came in as the leader and seconded his stand for the national affirmation of Quebec. He teamed up with Charland, Roy and Turp.

Bouchard never put aside the ideas he had promoted for the last four years and in the party manifesto, *Un nouveau parti pour l'étape décisive.* The European model and the possibility of some common political institutions with Canada were still in the back of his mind. As soon as he came back from his convalescence, he began to think about a proposal and a new question. He believed that he had the answer to the concerns expressed in the commissions, an exercise he found positive.

Because Bouchard strongly believed that public opinion should determine the political agenda, he decided to work quietly with that in mind. "People don't want the status quo. They want deep changes. At the same time, they want to do it in a certain way, with some formal assurances. We have to take that into account," he said at the time. How? "We're discussing all these ... a new project ... It is a sovereignist project, it's not a federalist project," he answered, sparing details. "Changing the question is not enough," he concluded. "For me, it is not a question of wording because people will always see clearly, will always see what is essential ... It takes some elements that don't appear in [the project] for the moment."

The work of the commissions was not over. A national commission, set up to listen to provincial organizations, was ready to begin sitting on March 22. The PQ, the Bloc, the ADQ and the presidents of all the regional commissions were there. Bouchard, who represented his party at the first meeting, upstaged Parizeau with his call for a referendum *"au plus sacrant"* (as fast as bloody possible) but Parizeau didn't seem to mind. The two men were in unison. At their joint press conference, the first one since the election, Bouchard and Parizeau spoke with one voice, each of them delicately opening the door to compromise. An economic union would have to follow not precede sovereignty, they repeated. The referendum would have to be held as soon as possible, preferably in 1995, they added, and the question should be "sovereignist and clear." But Bouchard again gave some hints about where his reflections were heading by talking of the virtues of a "partnership" with Canada and of the Maastricht Treaty.[18]

The harmony in the sovereignist camp didn't last long. During the six days of hearings, the idea that there was no rush and that a defeat would be devastating resurfaced with insistence. On March 26, Parizeau himself admitted that Quebecers were not yet ready to vote in favour of sovereignty. But he added that "all possible efforts should be made so they could be ready before very long."[19]

The day after, his deputy Bernard Landry sent his boss a blunt message. If Quebecers were not ready to vote Yes now, it was highly unlikely they would be more ready in June. "I don't want to be the second officer of the light brigade that was exterminated in twenty minutes in Crimea because of the irresponsibility of its commanders," he said, referring to the Battle of Balaklava where the commanders led the British troops to their death.[20]

The pressure on Parizeau to delay the referendum until the fall reached its peak. In the backrooms, it was intense. His MNAs, his cabinet colleagues and his regional representatives were all pressing him. On March 31, at a joint strategy meeting of the Bloc and the PQ held at the Delta Hotel in Montreal, the issue was again the subject of discussion. Bouchard and Parizeau were present. The Bloc leader informed his counterpart vis-à-vis of the message he wanted to deliver to his party during its convention, beginning the next Friday. It was then decided that the referendum would be postponed.

On April 5, in front of the Chamber of Commerce of Lévis, Parizeau announced with a grim face that the referendum would be held in the fall. He didn't set a date, but the government was working in high gear to get ready for an early referendum. After having stuck to his guns for so long, he was forced to make a public retreat. His anger would increase in the days to come, especially on April 7.

On that day, Bouchard opened the first Bloc convention in five years with a political torpedo. "[Quebecers] don't wish to say No to sovereignty in a referendum that would rush them and not answer their questions. They are ready to say Yes to a rallying project. The sovereignist project has to quickly take a sharp turn that will bring it closer to Quebecers and will open a credible path to the future for new Quebec-Canada relations," he said in front of about 1,300 delegates.[21]

He then began to describe what an economic union should look like. "Our fellow citizens want to give the Quebec-Canada economic union a more fully worked-out basis. In view of the magnitude of the common economic space, we have to reflect further on how to consolidate it. It is important to seriously examine the opportunity of a framework of common institutions, even of a political nature."

Referring to the Bloc and the PQ manifestoes, he said that the new economic partnership between both countries could be the result of an overall agreement that would establish management mechanisms, such as a parliamentary conference that would act as a discussion forum. "Made up of representatives delegated by both sovereign states, this assembly would deliberate on subjects of common interest. It could be conceivable that the conference's decision would be the result of proposals elaborated and submitted by a community council made up of ministers from the two states." This architecture, he added, would be completed by a secretariat and a tribunal that would act as a dispute-settlement mechanism. In the long run, it could make a place for bipartite administrative commissions on specific matters. He emphasized that the European model and the Maastricht Treaty were his inspiration.

Jacques Parizeau, who was in the room for this speech, had no choice but to applaud. After the strategy meeting of March 31, he knew that his ally wanted to change the focus of the referendum debate to echo the concern of participants at the commissions who were asking questions about what would happen to the economic union with Canada. He knew that Bouchard intended to elaborate on the common institutions and the content of the offer to English Canada mentioned in the draft bill. What Parizeau didn't know was that Bouchard would present this elaboration as a change in direction. Nor did he know that Bouchard would insistently advocate common political institutions, something Parizeau has never believed in.

Parizeau was not the only one handed a *fait accompli*. The Bloc delegates, who had prepared for the convention by discussing all sorts of issues, were not consulted. Their opinion was sought at the last minute during the Sunday plenary session. The party tabled an emergency resolution to study Bouchard's proposal further. The rules of order limited the number of interventions and little was left to chance. The microphones were monopolized by the party's big names, including Bouchard. Nevertheless, he had to reassure his members because many were left with the impression that he was turning back the clock and wanted to resuscitate the 1980 sovereignty-association proposal. He insisted that Quebecers would vote first on sovereignty and then make an offer to Canada. "If English Canada says No, the worst that can happen is we are a sovereign country," he said with irony.[22] The Bloc members, who never vote on a program and are more faithful to Bouchard than to anything else, followed him. They agreed to create a working group that would elaborate a clearer proposal. Only a handful of the participants expressed their dissent.

Only the Bloc MPs were aware of what was looming. They had been informed and consulted during a special caucus meeting the week before. But Parizeau saw the details of the speech at the same time as reporters, less than half an hour before Bouchard began to speak. For the PQ leader, it was a public blow, the equivalent of a reprimand on the way things were going. During the days that followed Bouchard's speech, PQ officials did everything to minimize his statement, saying there was no change of direction.

But Bouchard insisted it was a *virage,* a sharp turn, adding more or less subtle warnings to Parizeau. "He is the Quebec premier, he's in charge of a government, he just got elected with a majority. He has an extremely big margin of manoeuvre. But margins of manoeuvre are never absolute in politics. That's obvious. It's obvious that Monsieur Parizeau works with partners, works with public opinion." Bouchard continued to cast doubt on the referendum date, three days after Parizeau had announced its delay. "What I know is that the referendum should be held—should be held, if possible—in 1995. If possible means, if we can set up the winning conditions for a victory," he said to the press.[23]

He acknowledged that he didn't have Parizeau's support for his *virage.* But he also said he hadn't asked for his approval because he had to save something of substance for the party members. Bouchard spoke with the confidence of a person holding a winning hand. "We have no doubt that [Parizeau] will agree on the essential aspects of the proposal since he has himself recognized this week that we need time to readjust the project until next fall."

The Bloc leader denied pinning Parizeau against a wall. He said that his proposal would be one among others, but the answer he expected was clear. "Monsieur Parizeau has my full support and since he himself has not resolved what the ultimate decision will be, I have to wait before giving any unconditional agreement. I will not sign any blank cheque to anyone."

On Sunday, while Bouchard was making his closing speech at the convention, Parizeau was in Quebec City for the launch of a province-wide consultation on the education system. At the following press conference, he felt the need to remind Bouchard who was in charge. "There is one matter on which there must be no confusion—I am the premier of Quebec," he said.[24]

"The Bloc Québécois has the right to elaborate post-referendum scenarios, but one thing is clear. After a Yes vote in the referendum, the relations between a sovereign Quebec, a country named Quebec, and a country named Canada, will depend on two big actors, two big players: the government of Quebec and the government of Canada," he added.[25]

He repeated that 1995 would be a referendum year and he invited people to be cautious in the face of new ideas. "Every time somebody has a good idea, or thinks they have had a good idea, I hope we won't start saying there's a new twist because we'll all end up with a sore neck."[26]

He made clear that he would never accept a proposal that would make accession to sovereignty dependent on the answer of English Canada as was the case in 1980 when the PQ government asked for a mandate to negotiate and promised to consult the population again on the result.

The next day, both Parizeau and Bouchard had to attend a meeting in Montreal with the Partners for Sovereignty, a coalition of unions and popular organizations representing about one million people. Prior to the meeting, Parizeau went ahead with a speech in Laval. At the end, he met the press and admitted there was a "squabble in the sovereignist camp on a certain number of ideas and objectives." Trying to build bridges, he attributed the disagreement to the dynamism of the coalition. For him, it was a proof that sovereignists were reflecting on Quebec's future. He said that he favoured common institutions with Canada but that such an offer would have to come only after the referendum and that he doubted that Canada would accept an offer for common political institutions. "It takes two to tango," he said.[27]

Bouchard, for his part, went on the radio. In an interview with Michel Lacombe, of the French CBC's *Le Midi 15* program, he threatened to let Parizeau down if the referendum appeared doomed to failure at the outset. "If there's one thing I don't want, that I don't wish, it's to participate in a referendum campaign that would surely lead us to a defeat," he said.

"You just said to Monsieur Parizeau, if I understand well: if you hold the referendum when we know we're going to lose, I won't be with you?" asked Lacombe.

"I didn't say that, I didn't say that. At least, I haven't said it yet," Bouchard replied.

In the afternoon, the meeting with the Partners for Sovereignty went ahead, but the two men maintained their positions and avoided the press afterwards. The rift was plain. Bouchard left for a one-week holiday. Parizeau returned to Quebec City and started, the next day, to pour oil on the troubled waters. "For the moment, some believe that a turn has to be taken on certain things. Others believe, on the contrary, that there is no reason to turn. This will be discussed. But, fundamentally, the answer, I believe, will be found when all of us react, after April 19, the day the national commission will table its report." [28]

In delaying his response to Bouchard, Parizeau gave himself time to calm down his caucus and Cabinet, which had been divided by Bouchard's statements. In relying on the national commission report, he found a face-saving device and a way to adjust his position to the Bloc leader's. But he made clear to his caucus that there was one thing he would never accept: a dilution of Quebec's powers as an independent country.

The Quest for the Soft Sovereignists

Bouchard's gamble was a big one. The word *virage* caught the public's imagination, but when the Bloc leader talked about a turn, it was clear he wasn't thinking about his own dream. He had always advocated an economic and political association with Canada, one inspired by the European Union model. Before his April 7 speech, he never really gave details on the kind of institutions he envisaged but the canvas was there.

What Bouchard put forward looked a bit like the superstructure advocated for a while by former premier Robert Bourassa, but with two important distinctions. The common political institution, the parliamentary conference, would not be elected and its powers would be limited. Bourassa had proposed an elected Parliament with fiscal and legislative powers. Bouchard preferred to say that he took his inspiration from his hero, René Lévesque. But Lévesque didn't endorse the idea of common political institutions. In his White Paper published in 1979, he suggested offering Canada an economic association with a limited number of institutions to implement the treaty.

However, "the government of Quebec doesn't believe that it is opportune to propose the establishment of a parliamentary assembly. It judges that it is preferable that the members of the community council remain, politically accountable to their respective Parliament," he wrote in *La nouvelle entente Québec-Canada*. "If the rest of Canada proposed an interparliamentary assembly, made up of members chosen among elected MPs of the member states' Parliaments, the government of Quebec would have no objection to looking at this proposal," he elaborated. Bouchard distinguished himself from

Lévesque on another front. He always made sovereignty the prereq-
uisite to any negotiations with Canada. Lévesque had offered the
opposite course: negotiations first, sovereignty later. According to
Bouchard, it was an error.

With all this in mind, a question emerges. Did Bouchard turn on
April 7 or did he impose a turn on his partners? One year earlier, in
an interview with the *Toronto Star*, he was clear about who should
make an offer. "I would like to be on the receiving end of the
proposal," he told Edison Stewart.[29] In 1995, his point of view had
changed. To reassure Quebecers who wanted to know how Quebec-
Canada relations would look in the future, he concluded it was
necessary to let them know, before the referendum, the kind of offer
that Quebec would make to Canada. He stressed however that the
negotiations would only begin after a Yes vote. The question would
be on sovereignty accompanied by an offer of association to the rest
of Canada. No guarantee of association would be attached to it.

This approach rests on Bouchard's old belief that a vote in favour
of sovereignty would give Quebecers the bargaining power they
needed to force English Canada to make a decision. "The whole thing
is about giving the people of Quebec bargaining power, a real change
in dynamics where any proposal coming out from a sovereign Quebec would have to be considered very favourably and quite seriously
by the rest of Canada." [30]

The real turning, in terms of content, was therefore difficult for
Parizeau and most hardline sovereignists to swallow. In 1980 Parizeau had disagreed with Lévesque's sovereignty-association strategy but, as a faithful soldier, he had still campaigned alongside the
leader. In 1984, he quit the PQ because he couldn't support the *beau
risque* endorsed by Bouchard. He also distanced himself from
Lévesque's successor and Bouchard's friend, Pierre Marc Johnson,
who put sovereignty aside in favour of the concept of national affirmation.

Parizeau always promoted a clear *indépendantiste* stance and refused to flirt with compromises that he found unrealistic. Since his
return to the helm of the PQ, the hardline sovereignists have stuck
to the idea of an economic partnership between an independent
Québec and Canada that can be administered through institutions
similar to NAFTA's. For Parizeau, it was not at all a question of
political institutions like the parliamentary conference advocated by
Bouchard.

Bouchard's statements could be seen as a waking call for sovereignists, intended to tell them that they needed a softer stand to avoid a crushing defeat. Quebecers want changes but not a rupture. The problem with Bouchard was his method. The way he chose to manage the *virage* left the impression of a power struggle. By publicly disavowing his ally and casting doubt on his leadership, Bouchard pushed Parizeau into a corner, letting him know he wouldn't tolerate being ignored. It was as if Bouchard was saying, "I know better and I can say what I want because if I don't have the official power, I have the popular support and you need me."

In the English press, the reaction was immediate. A number of commentators were quick to recall Bouchard's "betrayal" of Mulroney. In the French press, some editorialists, like *La Presse*'s Alain Dubuc, defended the same stance. Others saw the gesture as one meant to push the PQ down the road to sovereignty-association or were convinced that it was proof of Bouchard's political ambitions. Finally, his gesture was understood as a way to broaden the sovereignist coalition, in particular in the direction of Mario Dumont and the ADQ members, a move that Parizeau could hardly make himself without doing an about-turn.

The Extended Hand
It was odd to see Bouchard building bridges to Dumont and the ADQ when two weeks earlier, at the national commission, Bouchard hadn't hesitated to attack Dumont. He didn't criticize his constitutional stand based on the European model, but his imprecision on the way to get there. And six months earlier, the two men had been at daggers because, shortly before the provincial election, Bouchard had agreed to go to the Rivière-du-Loup riding to campaign against Dumont.

Now the wind had changed. The opening Dumont was waiting for came with the *virage*. After Bouchard's speech, Dumont said that the Bloc leader was heading in the right direction and let it be understood he was open to an approach. His team called the Bloc to get more information about the nature of the offer to Canada. The Bloc proposal was similar in many areas to the ADQ's constitutional position. The ADQ's proposal is premised on a council of ministers, a secretariat or commission, a dispute-settlement mechanism, a monetary union, and a free circulation of people, goods, services and capital between Quebec and Canada.

But, contrary to the two other parties, the ADQ advocates an elected common Parliament with limited and specific jurisdictions. It elaborates that any bill would have to be initiated by the council of ministers. The ADQ also called for some common services, like the post office and defence. The two countries would have equal representation on the council of ministers. In the common Parliament, Quebec would have 25 per cent of the seats.

The main difference between the ADQ's plan and the Bloc's was in the sequence of events. The ADQ suggested a referendum question that made an offer to Canada on the basis of the European model. The ADQ also wanted to begin negotiations right away. If the negotiations failed, then Quebec would become sovereign, it said.

Bouchard, despite his public stance against Dumont, kept the door open to discussions. After the ADQ phone call, the leader's main advisers began informal talks that lasted about three weeks.

Parizeau, for his part, was waiting for the national commission's report. On April 19, as expected, the commission stated that sovereignty was "the only option able to answer Quebecers' aspirations." It added: "Once it is achieved, sovereignty will signal for Quebec a new beginning in a partnership with Canada that does not eventually exclude some form of political union. The national commission recommends that the Quebec government and the draft bill indicate that a sovereign Quebec could propose and negotiate common, mutually advantageous political institutions when circumstances so permit." [31]

In the end, Parizeau was able to save face. He had a justification for following Bouchard. The people had spoken. "At first glance it seems to me that this approach offers the grounds of common agreement for several forces in the camp for change," he said. "For my part, I find [in this report] my convictions and my struggle. It seems to also have an echo of the proposals made recently by Lucien Bouchard." [32]

However, he stayed cautious, allowing himself about 10 days before he made a definite statement. He wanted to consult his party, his MNAs and his cabinet. Contrary to the Bloc, the PQ has detailed structures and a long tradition of activism. Members do not only follow their leader, they often challenge him. The premier could not go around them.

On April 22, in Montreal, Parizeau announced the end of his public feud with his main ally. "The squabble is over. The report of the national commission has reconciled us, and Mr. Bouchard and I will conduct the referendum campaign hand in hand," he told reporters after a speech to delegates at a convention of municipalities. "The association with the rest of Canada is inescapable on certain points, desirable on others and could be contemplated on still others. Starting from there, we can all take the turnaround together." [33]

The day after, he went even further after a six-hour meeting with his caucus at a Quebec City hotel. The formal proposals for an economic and political association with Canada will be known before the referendum, he said. They would take the form of a treaty between two sovereign countries, but sovereignty would not depend on Canada's answer.

With the support of his caucus, Parizeau brought the rest of his party and his other allies on board. The following Wednesday, he got the approval of his riding presidents. On the Friday, it was the Partners for Sovereignty's turn to be persuaded by Bouchard and Parizeau. A Léger & Léger poll published by the *Globe and Mail* proved to be helpful. It showed that 53 per cent of Quebecers would vote in favour of sovereignty if it were coupled with economic association.

During Parizeau's consultations at the end of April, Dumont and Bouchard's advisers were still in touch on an informal basis. But they noted that they had to change gear and serious negotiations had to begin to pave the road to a real coalition, something that could not go ahead without PQ participation.

The PQ no longer had any problems coming on board and the advisers to the three party leaders started working out a common position. Bouchard was represented by his special adviser Pierre-Paul Roy and his chief of staff Gilbert Charland. Parizeau delegated his two special advisers, Jean-François Lisée and Hubert Thibault. Dumont asked Jacques Gauthier, chairman of the ADQ constitutional commission, and his adviser André Néron to act on his behalf. For more than a month, they met regularly. By the beginning of June, they had hammered out an agreement in principle.

By that time, Parizeau had already announced that a new question would be drafted that would make reference to an offer of "partnership" with Canada. He had indicated at the end of May that a new draft bill would be tabled in the fall. It would describe the offer of association and indicate the time limit to reach an agreement. He outlined in front of the PQ national council the main elements of the proposal, showing how far he was ready to go to get a compromise. On top of a council of ministers, a tribunal and a commission, he endorsed for the first time ever the creation of a joint political body; that is, a non-elected parliamentary assembly.

By this point, the public tension between Bouchard and Parizeau had calmed down. Then Bouchard slipped again. On June 1, he expressed doubt about the closure of nine hospitals in the Montreal area, an issue that was already a hot potato for the government. The incident was symptomatic of the Bloc's critical stance on the PQ government. In private, Bouchard's staff seemed almost contemptuous of Parizeau and his team. At the Bloc convention in April, activists said openly that the PQ should govern and leave the sovereignty battle to the Bloc. This new public criticism could have sparked a real controversy, considering the public was clearly against the closures.

But Parizeau was able to defuse the incident by saying that Bouchard was emotional because he was addressing the medical team that had saved his life. In fact, this statement wasn't true, but Bouchard seemed to get the message that he should mind his own business. He didn't comment again.

The New Agreement on Sovereignty

Both men had more important things to do than feud: an agreement in principle between Bouchard, Parizeau and Dumont was almost ready. On Friday, June 9, they presented it to the press.

The three men agreed that Quebecers would be asked, during a referendum in 1995, to decide to make Quebec a sovereign state and to formally propose to Canada a new economic and political partnership. After a Yes vote, the National Assembly would be empowered to proclaim sovereignty and the government would have the obligation to offer Canada a treaty proposal to establish the new partnership.

The document stated that the negotiations should last only one year, unless the National Assembly decided differently. If the talks were going smoothly, the legislature would proclaim sovereignty after the conclusion of the treaty. If not, it could proclaim sovereignty as soon as it saw fit.

The three men took for granted that international trade rules would apply to Quebec and ensure access to foreign markets, including Canada's. Quebec would keep the Canadian currency but, considering the extent of the economic relation, the leaders would prefer to conclude a partnership treaty. In addition to dividing assets and debt, the treaty would define the nature and the rules of the common institutions.

A council, with an equal number of ministers from both countries, should be established with a secretariat and a tribunal to settle disputes.

The ministers would have the powers to enforce the treaty, but their decisions would have to be unanimous. Each party would have a veto.

A parliamentary assembly would be formed of delegates from both legislatures. It would make recommendations, hold consultations, adopt resolutions but would have no legislative powers. Quebec would have 25 per cent of the seats and Canada, 75 per cent.

This partnership would oversee the customs union, the monetary union, manpower mobility, citizenship, and the free flow of people, goods, services and capital. In acknowledgement of the ADQ's position, the three leaders added that the two states could also cooperate on issues such as internal trade, international trade, international representation, transport, defence, financial institutions, fiscal and budgetary policies, environmental protection, policing the illegal traffic in arms and drugs, the postal service, and so on.

The big novelty was the proposal of a monitoring committee for the negotiations, an idea put forward by the ADQ. It would be formed by high-profile individuals chosen by the three parties. This committee would participate in the choice of the chief negotiator, would send an observer to the negotiations, would advise the government on the talks and would inform the public on the process and its results.

All three men had made compromises in their initial positions to achieve this agreement. Parizeau accepted more powers for the common institutions, the establishment of political bodies and the creation of a monitoring committee to oversee his government during the negotiations. Bouchard set his mind on a firm date for the referendum and backed the idea of unequal representation at the common Parliament. Dumont accepted a nonelected common Parliament without fiscal and legislative powers and, most important, he agreed to make sovereignty the inescapable first step.

During the following weekend, the three leaders had to consult the main bodies of their parties to consolidate their accord. Dumont was first to meet his general council. He succeeded in overcoming the mistrust in Parizeau expressed by his troops and got their approval. Bouchard followed with a caucus meeting, and Parizeau with an encounter with his caucus and national executive. In all cases, they met no hurdles. All this opened the door for the signing ceremony on June 12 at the Château Frontenac.

The three-party agreement was a turning point for the sovereignists. For the first time in months, they were speaking with one voice. The moment was important because it gave them a head start before the summer. They looked united and had something to put on the table. For once, Parizeau didn't have to check his back and proved he could show flexibility. Dumont, with his small party, was able to get a hand on the steering wheel. For Bouchard, it meant he had entered the last stretch. His only reason to be in politics, his "last battle"—the referendum on sovereignty—was nearly a reality.

10

The Bloc's Future

The Bloc is Bouchard. But Bouchard is ... Bouchard. After being pushed to create his own party, Bouchard became and remained the Bloc's only pivotal force.

At first, he was put off by the idea of creating a party. He had freed himself of party discipline and saw it as a trap he wanted to avoid. For years he was a reluctant leader, refusing to manage the conflicts in his small caucus, participating without enthusiasm in fundraising. Like the ancient tribunes, he preferred to be in the spotlight, alone, using his speaking ability to rouse popular support.

During the past five years, the Bloc may have acquired all the attributes of a real party — members, money, MPs, organizers. But it also has peculiar characteristics. It has no real program other than sovereignty, and one aim — to die as fast as possible afterwards. In addition, it relies entirely on its leader. With Bouchard gone, the Bloc would quickly wilt.

In fact, the Bloc still looks more like a movement bound by its veneration for the leader and the pursuit of a single mission than a true party. In 1992, on the eve of the Charlottetown Accord, the Privy Council Office asked for an analysis of the strengths and weaknesses of the Bloc. The confidential report underlined the way the Bloc was like a movement and the difficulties it was creating in a traditional political dynamic. "The purpose of movements is inherently moral rather than political: the cause they advocate is presented, often explicitly, in terms of a choice between right and wrong, rather than (as with political parties) better and worse, or as competing but equally legitimate alternatives." Simplicity, moral fervour and shared myths are their trademark. "Historic conspiracies are a frequent but not invariable aspect of such myths," noted the author, Christine Hewett. She added that movements often begin because of a "sense of exclusion or alienation ... widely shared" by the members and the followers.

This analysis has been confirmed with time. When the Meech Lake Accord was rejected, the Bloc could focus on this rejection and promote sovereignty as the means of restoring the pride and honour of Quebecers. Since the last election, Bouchard has constantly reminded people that a Yes vote would be the best antidote to Chrétien's plans "to finish the job of 1982" and to start a massive centralist attack on Quebec's powers.

As a leader, Bouchard personifies his cause. He has resigned from a position of power on a question of principle. Despite his contradictions, the historical errors in his speeches, the ungenerous motives he attributes to his opponents, people believe in his sincerity. They believe he speaks from the heart when he makes emotional pleas to Quebecers to refuse to be crushed or draws a dark picture of Quebec's future if the No side wins. Parizeau, on the contrary, calls for a reasoned choice, refuses to pronounce the word *defeat* and envisages its repercussions publicly. Once, he even asked Quebecers to stop whining and blaming others for their difficulties. But Bouchard is popular; not Parizeau.

In 1995, on the eve of a new referendum campaign, the Bloc has kept many of the characteristics of a movement. Bouchard is still the pivotal force, and the objective is still sovereignty to restore pride, honour and the ownership of destiny. Once Bouchard is gone or the referendum is successfully settled, the Bloc itself, relying as it does on its leader and its mission, is likely to disappear.

In the case of a Yes vote, the picture is clear. The Bloc will stay during the transition period, until Quebec has proclaimed its sovereignty and stopped paying taxes to Canada. After that, it will dissolve. During this time, it will have lost its official opposition status, not because Parliament will have stripped it away, but because some MPs will quit. All of them came to Ottawa to help realize sovereignty, but many have become disillusioned under the iron-clad discipline imposed by Bouchard and his associates. Frustrated at being treated like children, some will quit as soon as the vote is over. They have no interest in staying. If, as Bouchard expects, Jean Chrétien calls an election to have a mandate to answer a Yes vote, the Bloc will run in order to get elected. It will fight for the referendum result to be respected and will disappear when the issue is resolved.

In the case of a No vote for sovereignty, the Bloc will be forced to soul search. Bouchard has always said that the caucus will meet and then decide what it should do. The Bloc MPs who are frustrated by party discipline would be likely to leave along with the idealists whose dream would be shattered.

Some Bloc MPs would stay on for the remainder of their mandate. A scenario in which all of them would resign *en masse* is not favoured by many MPs, including House leader Michel Gauthier. "No matter what the referendum result is, the decision of the Bloc should be the result of a very large consulting process with voters and activists. If we lose, for example, we would be in the middle of a mandate. Do we have the right, like that, the 53, to resign and create a terrible political vacuum? Do we have the right to do that or should we see what our militants and the citizens want?" In Gauthier's mind, the political context will be the determinant and the decision will have to ensue from a large consensus.

On a more global basis, the question of the maintenance of a party after a No will be asked. Pressures will mount to keep the Bloc in Ottawa to defend Quebec interests and to represent the sovereignist portion of the population. A Léger & Léger poll published in the *Globe and Mail* in October 1994 indicated that some Quebecers were beginning to become complacent about having the Bloc as the opposition. Between October 15 and 19, the polling firm asked a sample of 1,007 Quebecers whether they agreed that the Bloc MPs should stay on if the No side won the referendum. In the sample as a whole, 65 per cent of respondents answered Yes; among Francophones, this figure was 71 per cent.[1]

Bouchard, at the time, was worried, fearing that Quebecers could decide to support the Bloc instead of sovereignty. He reacted quickly. At the Bloc's November general council, he warned Quebecers that they should not pursue a mirage. The Bloc could never be a substitute for a real political affirmation — in other words, sovereignty. "Quebecers should not think," he said, "that the Bloc Québécois is an accessory that comes with federalism or with sovereignty."[2]

But the need for a Quebec party would be felt, no matter what. Even Bouchard admits it now. "I don't rule out that the Bloc — I don't talk about the individuals — be subject to pressure to continue, no matter what happens, because Quebecers don't recognize themselves in the Liberals."

"Even if the answer to the referendum is No, the sovereignist option has to be kept alive and that means that we will need, on the federal scene, somebody to represent the Quebec nationalist trend. Momentarily, this trend would have to defend more traditional Quebec autonomist positions. A No doesn't mean that we desert the fight for Quebec powers. We will continue to revindicate new powers for Quebec. It's there that the Bloc takes all its importance and its *raison d'être*, forcing Canada to give new powers to Quebec. So the strategy of being there is valuable even if the sovereignist option is defeated by Quebecers," underlines Denis Monière, who tried to create this kind of party in 1984.

"It is not because a referendum will have taken place, that [the Bloc MPs] will disappear. Most of them will transform their approach to adopt a deep nationalistic attitude. The question is: does the Bloc have a future as a federalist party, by necessity not of conviction, to defend Quebec interests? There will be a game played because the Liberals will stay the same ... as long as Jean Chrétien is there," notes Conservative Senator Jean-Claude Rivest, a former adviser to Bourassa.

But it is almost certain that a party of this kind will be promised a marginal role, like the Ralliement Créditiste of Réal Caouette, which dwindled in the 1970s and finally disapeared.

Where will Bouchard be in all of this? He will be gone. After almost leading the sovereignist movement in the spring of 1995, he will have no interest in staying in Ottawa after a No vote. If it's a Yes, he may stay on for a while but even that is not certain. In the spring of 1995 in the House, Bouchard often looked bored, more interested in what was going on in Quebec City than in Ottawa. When asked about his future, he often mentioned that he could resume his law practice and have a quieter life with his wife, who doesn't like politics, and his children. But the call of politics might be tough to ignore. Bouchard himself admits that being his own master has made him discover a pleasant aspect of the game. The power.

"I don't relish the bad aspects of politics but I'm beginning to like it much more. Honestly, there is something in politics that you don't have anywhere else and I feel much better now in my own party than in a different party. I'm probably someone who has not the capacity to work under someone else. Obviously, it didn't work, even with my friend. This is my party, the party I created and I enjoy working with the team we have composed," he told Valerie Pringle, host of CTV's *Canada AM* on September 22, 1994.

After his brush with death, some family members tried to discourage him from returning to public life. Yet he came back. It was not only because of his sense of mission, but also because he was hooked. "I discovered that I like politics," he said to Pringle in another interview on February 22, 1995. His convalescence was an opportunity for him to reflect on his future and his life in politics.

He began his political career believing it was going to be short. "Even when I started the Bloc, I saw it as something temporary, a way to give something a push before returning to my law practice." Here was the perfect opportunity to quit and resume a quieter life. "I think people would have understood. And if not, I would have felt comfortable deciding to quit politics to take care of my family and resume my profession," he admits three months after his release from hospital. "I decided that if I was going to come back, it wouldn't be superficial, it wouldn't be a weak commitment. It would be a deliberate choice. In fact, for the first time in my life, I entered politics."

For Bouchard, the only political road that lies ahead after the referendum is the one to Quebec City. It is unlikely Bouchard would work the backrooms to oust Parizeau. He dislikes politics with a small *p*. It's not his style and he doesn't have the patience. But if others call upon him, the temptation could be great. "He will not take the job unless it's given to him. He will not graft to take it, will not knock somebody to take it," says one of his closest advisers. The only thing, again, that can persuade Bouchard to say No, is his family, particularly his wife.

Bouchard no longer hides the fact that he has reflected on the role of premier. Asked if he would like to have it, he answers that "it's like asking a bishop if he wants to become pope. All bishops dream of becoming the pope. The problem is that many are called but few are chosen ... But to answer seriously, it should first be possible. I'm not sure that it is possible. I'm not sure," he says.

"Is it because you're not ready to make the sacrifices it would require?"

"I've done a good part. Already, that's not bad."

"But it means more ..."

"Yeah, it is costly, it is costly. But if it is only to have the job, as Monsieur Parizeau says ..." Bouchard sighs. "You have to do something with it ... When I think about that, I think about it in these terms: What could I do, what more could I bring or what difference could I make? That's when I worry about the discrepancy between people's expectations and what I think I'm able to do."

*TEXT OF THE AGREEMENT
BETWEEN*

The Parti Québécois,
the Bloc Québécois and
the Action démocratique
du Québec

Ratified by

Messrs. Jacques Parizeau, Lucien
Bouchard and Mario Dumont

in Quebec city
June 12, 1995

A Common Project

Representing the Parti Québécois, the Bloc Québécois and the Action démocratique du Québec, we have reached agreement on a common project to be submitted in the referendum, a project that responds in a modern, decisive and open way to the long quest of the people of Québec to become masters of their destiny.

We have agreed to join forces and to coordinate our efforts so that in the coming Fall 1995 referendum, Quebecers will be able to vote for a real change: to achieve sovereignty for Québec and formally propose a new economic and political partnership with Canada, aimed among other things at consolidating the existing economic space.

The elements of this common project will be integrated in the bill that will be tabled in the Fall and on which Quebecers will vote on referendum day.

We believe that this joint project respects the wishes of a majority of Quebecers, reflects the historical aspirations of Québec, and embodies, in a concrete way, the concerns expressed before the Commissions on the future of Québec.

In this way, our joint project breaks with the Canadian status quo, rejected by the overwhelming majority of Quebecers. It is true to the aspirations of Quebecers for autonomy and enables Québec to become sovereign: to collect all of its taxes, pass all of its laws, sign all of its treaties. Our project also incorporates the wish of Quebecers to maintain a fair and flexible tie with our Canadian neighbours, in order to jointly manage the economic space, particularly by means of joint institutions, including institutions of a political nature. We are convinced that this proposal reflects both the interests of Québec and Canada, but we cannot of course predict the decision that Canadians will take in this regard.

Finally, our project responds to the oft-repeated wish in Québec that the referendum be capable of uniting as many Quebecers as possible on a clear, modern and open proposal.

The Referendum Mandate

Following a Yes victory in the referendum, the National Assembly will, on the one hand, be able to proclaim the sovereignty of Québec, and on the other hand, the government will have the duty of proposing to Canada a treaty on a new economic and political Partnership, so as to, among other things, consolidate the existing economic space.

The referendum question will contain these two elements.

Accession to Sovereignty

In the event that negotiations unfold in a positive fashion, the National Assembly will declare Québec's sovereignty after an agreement is reached on the Partnership treaty. One of the first gestures of a sovereign Québec will be the ratification of the Partnership treaty.

These negotiations will not go on for more than one year, unless the National Assembly decides otherwise.

In the event that negotiations prove to be fruitless, the National Assembly will be able to declare Québec sovereign upon short notice.

The Treaty

The new rules and the reality of international trade will enable a sovereign Québec, even without a formal Partnership with Canada, to have access to external markets, among which the Canadian one. A sovereign Québec could also, by its own choice, keep the Canadian dollar as its currency.

Nevertheless, given the volume and the diversity of trade between Québec and Canada and the extent of their economic integration, it will certainly be to the advantage of both States to sign a formal treaty of economic and political Partnership.

The treaty will be binding on the parties and will specify the appropriate measures for maintaining and improving the existing economic space. It will establish rules for division of federal assets and for managing the common debt. It will create the joint political institutions required to administer the new Economic and Political Partnership, and specify their rules of conduct. It will provide for the establishment of a Council, a Secretariat, an Assembly and a Dispute Resolution Tribunal.

The treaty will ensure in priority that the Partnership is capable of taking action in the following areas:

- customs union;
- free flow of goods;
- free flow of individuals;
- free flow of services;
- free flow of capital;
- monetary policy;
- labour mobility;
- citizenship.

Depending on the dynamics of the joint institutions, and the rhythm with which they wish to progress, nothing will prevent the two member States from reaching agreement in any other area of common interest, such as:

- in matters of internal trade, adapting and strengthening the provisions of the Inter-Provincial Trade Agreement;
- in matters of international trade (such as reaching common positions on the question of cultural exemption in the WTO and NAFTA);
- in matters of international representation (for example, the Council could decide, when useful or necessary, that the Partnership will speak with one voice within international organizations);
- in matters of transportation (to facilitate, for example, access to the two countries' airports or to harmonize highway, rail or interior marine transportation policies);
- in matters of defence policy (such as joint participation in peace-keeping operations or a coordinated participation in NATO and NORAD);
- in matters of financial institutions (such as defining regulations for chartered banks, security rules and rules of sound financial practices);
- in matters of fiscal and budgetary policies to maintain a dialogue to foster their compatibility;
- in matters of environmental protection in order to set objectives in the areas of cross-border pollution and the transportation and storage of dangerous goods;
- in matters of the fight against arms and drugs smuggling;
- in matters of postal services;
- in all other matters that the parties could consider of common interest.

Joint institutions
1) The Council
The Partnership Council, equally made up of Ministers from the two States, will have decision-making power with regard to the implementation of the treaty.

The Partnership Council's decisions should be unanimous, therefore each member would have a veto.

The Council will be assisted by a permanent secretariat. The Secretariat will serve as a working liaison between the governments and oversee the implementation of the Council's decisions. Upon the request of the Council or the Parliamentary Assembly, the Secretariat would produce reports on any subject relating to the application of the treaty.

2) The Parliamentary Assembly

A Parliamentary Assembly of the Partnership will be created, made up of Québec and Canadian members appointed by their respective Legislative Assemblies.

It will examine the draft decisions of the Partnership Council, and forward its recommendations. It could also pass resolutions on any aspect of their implementation, particularly after receiving the periodical reports on the state of the Partnership that would be produced by the Secretariat. It would hear, in public sessions, the heads of the bipartite administrative commissions responsible for the application of specific treaty provisions.

The composition of the Assembly will reflect the population distribution within the Partnership. Québec will hold 25% of the seats. Funding for the Partnership's institutions will be equally shared, except for the parliamentarians' expenses, for which each State will be responsible.

3) The Tribunal

A tribunal shall be set up to resolve disputes relating to the treaty, its implementation and the interpretation of its provisions. Its decisions will be binding upon the parties.

For its governing rules, we could draw from existing mechanisms, such as the NAFTA panel, that of the Inter-Provincial Trade Agreement or that of the World Trade Organization.

The Committee

An orientation and supervision committee will be set up for the negotiations. It will be made up of independent personalities agreed upon by the three parties (PQ, BQ, ADQ). Its composition will be revealed at the appropriate time. This committee:

1) will be involved in choosing the head negotiator;

2) will be able to assign an observer at the negotiation table;

3) will advise the government on the negotiations progress;

4) will inform the public on the negotiations process and outcome.

The democratic representatives of our three parties, having examined and signed the present agreement yesterday, June 12, 1995 —

the Action démocratique du Québec having met in Sherbrooke, the Bloc Québécois in Montreal, and the Parti Québécois in Quebec City — we sign today this common project and we invite all Quebecers to rally around it.

In witness whereof, we have signed,

Jacques Parizeau
President of the Parti Québécois

Lucien Bouchard
Leader of the Bloc Québécois

Mario Dumont
Leader of the Action démocratique du Québec

Endnotes

These notes refer only to published sources. Unattributed quotations are taken from interviews conducted by the author.

Introduction

1. Louis Balthazar, *Bilan du nationalisme au Québec* (Montreal: Éditions L'Hexagone, 1986), p. 100; Paul-André Linteau, René Durocher, Jean-Claude Robert and François Ricard, *Quebec Since 1930*, translated by Robert Chodos and Ellen Garmaise (Toronto: James Lorimer and Company, 1991), pp. 103–4.
2. Monière, *Pour la suite de l'histoire*, p. 114; *Canadian Parliamentary Guide*.
3. Vera Murray, *Le Parti québécois: De la fondation à la prise du pouvoir* (Éditions Cahiers du Québec — Hurtubise HMH, Coll. Science politique, 1976), p. 189–190.
4. André Bernard, "The Bloc Québécois," in *The Canadian General Elections of 1993* (Ottawa: Carleton University Press, 1994), p. 79.
5. Marcel Léger, *Le Parti Québécois* (Montreal: Ed. Québec-Amérique, 1986), p. 192.
6. Ibid., p. 197.
7. *Le Devoir*, October 15, 1982; *La Presse*, October 27, 1982.
8. *Le Devoir*, October 27, 1982.
9. Léger, *Parti québécois*, p. 222.
10. *Le Devoir*, October 3, 1983.

Chapter 1

1. Canadian Press, May 23, 1990.
2. *Le Devoir*, May 24, 1990.
3. *Le Devoir*, May 24, 1990.
4. *Le Devoir*, May 26, 1990.
5. Toronto *Star*, May 23, 1990, tape of press conference, May 22, 1990.
6. *Le Soleil*, May 23, 1990; *Le Devoir*, May 24, 1990.
7. Canadian Press, May 27, 1990.
8. Canadian Press, May 27, 1990; *Le Devoir*, May 28, 1990.
9. Toronto *Star*, May 28, 1990; Montreal *Gazette*, May 28, 1990.
10. *Le Soleil*, June 7, 1990.

11. *Le Soleil*, June 8, 1990.
12. Montreal *Gazette*, May 24, 1990.
13. *Le Soleil*, June 15, 1990.
14. *House of Commons Debates*, June 26, 1990.
15. Ibid.
16. *La Presse*, June 28, 1990.
17. Toronto *Star*, June 30, 1990.
18. Montreal *Gazette*, June 30, 1990; *La Presse*, June 28, 1990; *Le Devoir*, June 28, 1990.

Chapter 2
1. *Le Devoir*, May 26, 1990.
2. Montreal *Gazette*, May 23, 1990.
3. Ottawa *Citizen*, May 23, 1990.
4. Toronto *Globe and Mail*, May 18, 1991.
5. Michel Vastel, *Bourassa* (Montreal, Éditions de l'Homme, 1991), p. 29.
6. Léger & Léger data.

Chapter 3
1. "Federal Voters' Intentions," Léger and Léger poll.
2. Compilation of questions and MPs' statements between June 1991 and June 1993. From Canada, House of Commons, *Debates (Hansard)*. Parliament, Vol.II. Ottawa: Queen's Printer, 1991, 1993.
3. *Le Devoir*, January 28, 1991.
4. *Le Devoir*, January 31, 1991.
5. *Le Soleil*, April 9, 1991, *Le Devoir*, April 8, 1991.
6. "Table Showing Sovereignist Support," Léger and Léger.

Chapter 4
1. *La Presse*, October 26, 1990.
2. Bloc Québécois, *Vers le nécessaire rassemblement*, pp. 38–39.
3. Bloc Québécois, *Sommaire du Manifeste*, June 5, 1991, p. 3.
4. Bloc Québécois, *Vers le nécessaire rassemblement*, p. 39.
5. Ibid., p. 39.
6. Canadian Press, June 15, 1990.
7. Jean Fournier, *Plan stratégique du Bloc Québécois et plan d'action pour la Période de janvier à juin 1992*, p. 7.
8. Fournier, *Plan stratégique*, p. 7.
9. Lisée, *Le Naufrageur*, p. 504.

Chapter 5
1. Montreal *Gazette*, January 19, 1993.
2. Ottawa *Citizen*, January 12, 1993.
3. *Le Soleil*, March 29, 1993.
4. Schedule of activities 1992–93.

5. Montreal *Gazette*, February 11, 1993.
6. *La Presse*, March 8, 1993.
7. Toronto *Star*, March 8, 1993.
8. *La Presse*, March 22, 1993.
9. Montreal *Gazette*, February 11, 1993.
10. *La Presse*, March 8, 1993.
11. *Le Devoir*, March 22, 1993.
12. *Le Soleil*, March 29, 1993.
13. *Le Devoir*, May 13, 1993.
14. *Le Devoir*, June 21, 1993.
15. *Le Devoir*, March 25, 1993.
16. *La Presse*, March 15, 1993; *Le Devoir*, March 25, 1993.
17. *Le Devoir*, March 25, 1993.
18. *Le Devoir*, March 25, 1993.
19. *Le Devoir*, March 25, 1993.
20. *Le Devoir*, April 4, 1993.
21. *Le Devoir*, April 4, 1993.
22. *La Presse*, April 3, 1993.
23. *Le Soleil*, April 5, 1993.
24. *La Presse*, June 8, 1993.
25. *Le Soleil*, June 21, 1993.
26. *Le Devoir*, June 22, 1993.
27. *Le Devoir*, May 4, 1993.
28. *Le Devoir*, June 21, 1993.
29. Letter of intent.
30. Bloc Québécois, Electoral Budget Projection (memo), August 13, 1993.
31. Guide to the fundraising campaign.
32. Memo, October 1, 1993.
33. Media plan, August 16, 1993.
34. *La Presse*, Toronto *Globe and Mail*, September 9, 1993.
35. *La Presse*, October 2, 1993.
36. *Le Devoir*, September 21, 1993.
37. *Financial Post*, October 2, 1993.
38. Memo, September 30, 1993.
39. Montreal *Gazette*, October 2, 1993.
40. *La Presse*, October 2, 1993.
41. Montreal *Gazette*, September 29, 1993.
42. *Le Devoir*, September 30, 1993.
43. *La Presse*, September 11, 1993.
44. *The Gazette*, October 12, 1993.

Chapter 6

1. *Le Droit*, April 7, 1994.
2. *Le Devoir*, January 16, 1994.
3. Toronto *Star*, February 10, 1994.

4. Press conference, June 22, 1994.
5. *Maclean's*, June 13, 1994; *La Presse*, January 22, 1994; Vancouver *Sun*, February 4, 1994; Toronto *Globe and Mail*, March 11, 1994.

Chapter 7

1. Ekos poll taken between September 24 and 28, cited in *Le Devoir*, September 30, 1993: "Fifty-two per cent of Canadian respondents believe that the election of a large group of Bloc members would constitute a threat to Canadian unity."
2. Montreal *Gazette*, October 5, 1993; Canadian Press report in the Toronto *Globe and Mail*, October 6, 1993; *Le Droit*, October 6, 1993.
3. Canadian Press report in *Le Droit*, October 9, 1993.
4. Ottawa *Citizen*, August 26, 1993; *La Presse*, October 9, 1993; *La Presse*, September 18, 1993; *Journal de Montréal*, June 16, 1994.
5. Canadian Press report in *Le Droit*, January 24, 1994.
6. *Maclean's*, November 29, 1993.
7. *La Presse*, December 7, 1992; *La Presse*, January 18, 1993.
8. Canadian Press report in *Le Devoir*, April 19, 1993; Montreal *Gazette*, April 20, 1993.
9. Toronto *Star*, August 15, 1993.
10. Toronto *Star* interview, September 22, 1993.
11. *La Presse*, October 7, 1993.
12. *Le Devoir*, November 10, 1993.
13. Toronto *Star*, March 21, 1994.
14. Canadian Press report in the Montreal *Gazette*, March 10, 1994.
15. Ottawa *Sun*, March 1, 1994; Toronto *Sun*, March 8, 1994.
16. Toronto *Globe and Mail*, May 4, 1994; Canadian Press, May 3, 1994; Vancouver *Sun*, May 2, 1994.
17. *Maclean's*, May 16, 1994; Montreal *Gazette*, May 11, 1994.
18. Toronto *Star*, May 16, 1994; *Journal de Montréal*, May 16, 1994; Toronto *Globe and Mail*, May 17, 1994; *Le Devoir*, May 18, 1994; Montreal *Gazette*, May 19, 1994.
19. *Le Devoir*, May 18, 1994; Toronto *Globe and Mail*, May 26, 1994; Montreal *Gazette*, May 18, 1994.

Chapter 8

1. Bloc Québécois, *Un nouveau parti pour l'étape décisive*, p. 81.
2. *Le Devoir*, June 21, 1993.
3. *Le Devoir*, October 12, 1993.
4. *Le Devoir*, October 13, 1993.
5. *Le Devoir*, October 16, 1993.
6. Toronto *Globe and Mail*, October 8, 1993.
7. *La Presse*, October 13, 1993.
8. *Un nouveau parti pour l'étape décisive*, pp. 85-99; pp. 117-20.
9. *Un nouveau parti*, p. 92.

10. *Un nouveau parti*, p. 92.
11. *Le Devoir*, October 6, 1993; *Financial Post*, December 4, 1993.
12. *L'Actualité*.
13. Toronto *Globe and Mail*, May 24, 1990.

Chapter 9

1. Toronto *Globe and Mail*, August 4, 1994.
2. Presse Canadienne, August 4, 1994.
3. *Canada AM*, CTV, September 22, 1994.
4. Scrum, September 19, 1994.
5. Presse Canadienne, December 16, 1994.
6. *La Presse*, December 9, 1994.
7. *Le Soleil*, February 18, 1995.
8. Toronto *Globe and Mail*, February 22, 1995.
9. CTV, February 22, 1995.
10. CBC, February 21, 1995.
11. *Le Soleil*, February 20, 1995.
12. SRC, February 19, 1995.
13. CBC, February 21, 1995.
14. *Le Soleil*, February 20, 1995.
15. Press conference, February 22, 1995.
16. Ibid.
17. *Le Soleil*, March 9, 1995.
18. *Le Soleil*, March 3, 1994; *Le Devoir*, March 23, 1995.
19. *Le Devoir*, March 27, 1995.
20. *Le Devoir*, March 28, 1995.
21. Speech, Bloc convention, April 7, 1995.
22. Declaration, Plenary session, April 9, 1995.
23. Scrum, April 8, 1995.
24. Toronto *Star*, April 10, 1995.
25. *Le Soleil*, April 10, 1995.
26. *Le Soleil*, April 10, 1995.
27. *La Presse*, April 11, 1995.
28. *Le Devoir*, April 12, 1995.
29. Toronto *Star*, February 12, 1994.
30. Toronto *Globe and Mail*, April 29, 1995.
31. *La Presse*/Toronto *Globe and Mail*, April 20, 1995.
32. Montreal *Gazette*/*La Presse*, April 20, 1995.
33. *Le Devoir*, April 24, 1995.

Chapter 10

1. Toronto *Globe and Mail*, October 21, 1994.
2. Presse Canadienne, November 27, 1994.

Bibliography

Balthazar, Louis. *Bilan du nationalisme au Québec*. Montreal: L'Hexagone, 1986. 212 pp.

Bernard, André. "The Bloc Québécois," in *The Canadian General Election of 1993*. Ottawa: Carleton University Press, 1994. 205 pp.

Bloc Québécois. *Document de travail: énoncé de politique*. 1992. 29 pp.

———. *Guide de la campagne de financement électoral — Document préliminaire*. 1993.

———. *Le manifeste*. Tracy, 1991. 11 pp.

———. *Un nouveau parti pour l'étape décisive*. (Lettre de Lucien Bouchard). Montreal, 1993. 59 pp.

———. *Vers le nécessaire rassemblement des souverainistes à Ottawa*. Tracy, 1991. 41 pp.

Bouchard, Lucien. *On the Record*. Trans. Dominique Clift. Toronto: Stoddart, 1994.

———, ed. *Un nouveau parti pour l'étape décisive*. Sherbrooke: Fides, 1993. 122 pp.

Canadian Parliamentary Guide. Various editions.

Denis, Roch. *Québec, dix ans de crise constitutionnelle*. Montreal: VLB, 1990. 306 pp.

Fournier, Jean. *Plan stratégique du Bloc Québécois et plan d'action pour la période de janvier à juin 1992*. 1992.

Fournier, Pierre. *Autopsie du Lac Meech. La souveraineté est-elle inévitable?* Montreal: VLB, 1990. 214 pp.

Léger, Marcel. *Le Parti québécois. Ce n'était qu'un début …* Montreal: Québec-Amérique, 1986. 350 pp.

Linteau, Paul-André; Durocher, René and Robert, Jean-Claude. *Quebec: A History. 1867–1929*. Trans. Robert Chodos. Toronto: James Lorimer and Company, 1983. 602 pp.

————, and Ricard, François. *Quebec Since 1930*. Trans. Robert Chodos and Ellen Garmaise. Toronto: James Lorimer and Company, 1991. 632 pp.

Lisée, Jean-François. *The Trickster: Robert Bourassa and Quebecers. 1990–1992*. Trans. Robert Chodos, Simon Horn and Wanda Taylor. Toronto: James Lorimer and Company, 1994. 392 pp.

Monière, Denis. *Pour la suite de l'histoire. Essai sur la conjoncture politique au Québec*. Montreal: Québec-Amérique, 1982. 182 pp.

————, and Guay, Jean H. *La bataille du Québec — Premier épisode: les élections fédérales de 1993*. Montreal: Fides, 1994. 193 pp.

Murray, Vera. *Le Parti québécois de la fondation à la prise du pouvoir*. Montreal: Cahiers du Québec — Hurtubise HMH, Coll. Science politique, 1976. 242 pp.

Stratégem Inc. *Bloc Québécois — élections automne 1993 — Plan média*. 1993.

Vastel, Michel. *Bourassa*. Trans. Hubert Bauche. Toronto: Macmillan, 1991.

Index

ADQ. *See* Parti de l'Action démocratique du Québec
Amyot, Guy, 73
Aubry, Jacques, 53, 61

Bachand, Claude, 90, 95
beau risque, 8, 50, 84, 150
Beaudoin, Louise, 65, 82
Beaudoin-Dobbie Report, 36
Beaulne, François, 54
Bedard, Marc-André, 8, 15
Bégin, Paul, 7
Béland, Claude, 4, 5, 24, 40, 76
Bélanger-Campeau Commission, 22-24, 26, 35, 47, 57, 84
Bellehumeur, Michel, 88
Berger, Lucette, 53, 61, 70, 74
Bergeron, Stephan, 72
Bernier, Maurice, 88
Bernier, Raynald, 94
Bertrand, Jean-François, 143-44
Bibeau, Pierre, 28-29
Bill 150, 57, 58
Biron, Rodrigue, 8
Bissonnette, Michel, 42
Blais, Pierre, 8
Bloc Québécois: 1993 election candidates, 70-74; 1995 convention, 145-48; and aboriginal people, 119-21; caucus policy decisions, 117; and Charlottetown referendum, 63-68; concentration of power, 92; creation of party, 39-40, 47-55; cultural issues, 126-27; divided caucus, 36-46, 63; ethical issues, 127; foreign affairs, 127-28; founding convention, 54; and Francophone minorities, 117-18; free trade/trade liberalization, 110, 115, 121-22; future, 157-61; as group of independent MPs, 31, 32-46; and GST, 122-23; health issues, 100, 126; industrial policy, 122; and justice 124-25; labour issues, 125-26; manifesto, 52-53; mission statement, 26, 31, 37; MPs, 87-89; MPs rules of behaviour, 92-96; name of party, 17, 31; official opposition, 85-101; policy commission, 114-15, 121; relations with Parti Québécois, 39, 40, 49, 54-55, 59, 60, 61, 64-65, 67-69, 76-80, 117, 118, 121, 132-49, 152, 154; shadow cabinet positions, 93; and social programs, 123-34; social-democratic principles, 116, 121, 123; and sovereignty, 115-16, 128-31, 129-30, 145-46, 149-50; supporters, 76-77, 79, 83; women candidates, 71-72. *See also* federal election campaign of 1993
Blouin, Claude, 54
Boileau, Pierre, 7, 77, 132
Bolduc, Roch, 29
Bonin, Gilles, 86
Bouchard, Benoît, 9, 11
Bouchard, Jacques, 6
Bouchard, Lucien, 6, 8, 10-11, 12; absenteeism, 35; against creation of party, 49, 51, 57; ambassadorship, 20-21; career as management negotiator, 4, 19-20; Chamber of Commerce meeting, 1-3; demanding leader, 90, 94; distrust of caucus, 44; early political leanings, 18-19; family background, 18; federal election campaign, 80-84; illness, 138; Laurier-Sainte-Marie byelection, 13-14, 15-16; *le virage*, 147, 149, 151; leader of non-partisan MPs, 13; Mulroney Cabinet minister, 21; and non-aligned group, 23-24; Quebec Bar meeting, 4; and rainbow coalition, 47, 60, 67-68; relations with Gérin, 38, 39-41, 44, 55; resignation from Conservative caucus, 1, 3, 5, 21-22; riding meeting, 3; rift with Parizeau, 143-49
Boudrault, Nicole, 53